paul gayler

a passion for cheese

paul gayler

a passion for cheese

more than 130 innovative ways to cook with cheese

with photographs by gus filgate

kyle books

This revised edition published 2007 by
Kyle Books, an imprint of
Kyle Cathie Limited
www.kylecathie.com

Distributed by National Book Network
4501 Forbes Boulevard, Suite 200,
Lanham, MD 20706
Phone (301) 459 3366

First published in 1998 by St. Martin's Press

ISBN 978 1 904920 59 5

Paul Gayler is hereby identified as the author of this work in
accordance with Section 77 of the Copyright, Designs and
Patents Act, 1988

Gayler, Paul.
A Passion for Cheese: More than 180 innovative ways to
cook with cheese/ Paul Gayler.
1. Cookery, Cheese.
Library of Congress Control Number: 2006939226

Home economy by Louise Pickford, assisted by Zoë Sharp
Styling by Penny Markham
Book design by Geoff Hayes

The publishers wish to thank Michael Day of the Huge
Cheese Company for his donation of the cheeses used in
the photographs, and the Guilde des Fromagers for
permission to reproduce their logo.

Photograph on page 2 shows Red Mullet on Baked Salad
Caprese with Basil & Olive Oil; photograph on page 6 shows
Lemon Blini with Ricotta & Raspberries.

contents

foreword

Cheese is a combination of man's ingenuity and one of Mother Nature's finest miracles, milk, and it never ceases to amaze me that from something so simple and so natural thousands of cheeses are made around the world. Each with their own unique flavor, character, and texture is a reflection of the soil, the grazing, the breed of animal, and the passion and skill of the cheesemaker and should be enjoyed first and foremost on its own with maybe a glass of wine and some wonderful local bread.

However, cheese is also one of the most versatile ingredients available to a chef or cook and can turn the simplest or most mundane dish into a gastronomic sensation. Imagine pasta without Parmigiano-Reggiano or French cuisine without their soft, aromatic goat cheeses or spicy Roquefort? Some dishes, like cheese on toast, cheese omelet or soufflé, can be made with almost any cheese. Others like Fondue or Greek salad rely on the unique texture and taste of specific cheeses so if the chef does not have an in-depth knowledge and understanding of the different cheeses the end result will fall well short of perfection when a substitute is used.

In the last 15 years I have seen endless cookery books and TV programs featuring recipes with cheese but most are simply old recipes revamped to sell another book. The choice of cheeses is seemingly arbitrary, often ill chosen, and simply demonstrates how little the writer cares or understands about how cheese interacts or marries with other ingredients. Too often generic names like "chevre" or blue cheeses are used, which in most cases is as pointless as saying fruit instead of apple, or lettuce instead of cos [Romaine] lettuce in a Caesar salad.

Paul Gayler however, is genuinely passionate about cheese and has taken time to create dishes that will bring out the best in the cheese or chosen cheeses that truly enhance the dish. Best of all he actually names the cheeses and offers alternatives, rather than using generic names, and has given a modern twist to some traditional dishes like Saltimbocca.

Paul brings to the book the same professionalism and enthusiasm that has won him the respect of his contemporaries in the highly competitive restaurant world and those who work with him in his kitchen at The Lanesborough in London. The layout and Paul's style of writing is straightforward, practical, and easy to follow, but is also imaginative, inspirational, and beautifully photographed, making it the perfect gift for anyone who loves cheese.

Juliet Harbutt
www.thecheeseweb.com

introduction

When I wrote A Passion for Cheese, I wanted to celebrate the remarkable variety of superb cheeses that had recently become available, and in particular the renaissance in farmhouse cheesemaking. I could never have imagined that, a decade later, the revolution would have continued apace, with even more cheeses appearing on the market and a whole new generation of specialist shops opening up.

Perhaps the biggest change in the way we eat now is that we are more interested in where our food comes from. Good restaurants make a point of sourcing local food and are proud to state its provenance on their menus. Many consumers like to shop at farmers' markets, where all the food is produced locally, or go direct to the farm to buy produce, which provides the opportunity to talk to the people who actually produce the food—a welcome change from the anonymity of the supermarket—and also to escape from industrialized, mass-produced ingredients and enjoy something with a little individuality.

Farmhouse cheese is one of the big success stories of local, artisan food. Small-scale cheese-makers tend to use milk from their own herd and make the cheese on-farm in their own dairy. It's the ideal product to sell locally—indeed, some soft cheeses have such a short shelf life that they have to be sold locally. Quality is all-important to small food producers, and the quality of cheese depends on the breed of animal, be it cow, sheep, or goat, the pasture on which it has grazed, and the skill of the cheesemaker. Because of this, we know when we buy farmhouse cheese that we are buying something truly special.

With the growth of artisan cheeses, more specialist cheese shops are opening up, and you can even shop on the internet, purchasing all your cheese by mail order. Supermarkets remain the least interesting place to buy cheese, ignoring smallscale cheesemakers, who can't produce the kind of quantities they require. I would like to see more done in future to give small producers the opportunity to sell their produce in local supermarkets. Perhaps because of the increasing number of cheeses available, we are now more willing to experiment with new varieties. Cow's milk cheese is perennially popular.but sales of goat cheese are on the increase. At the same time as the expansion of interest in local cheeses, Mediterranean cheeses have become more popular than ever, with classics such as Parmesan and mozzarella becoming staples to rival Cheddar and Stilton.

With such a wealth of wonderful cheeses accessible, the creative possibilities for cooking are endless. It seems to me that cheese's unique characteristics in cooking are too often overlooked. Why not pair blue cheese with white fish, or Cheddar with a lobster bisque? Use goat cheese to make a pesto sauce? Add Sage Derby to a stuffing for quail? These are just some of the unlikely-sounding combinations in this book that have turned out to be real winners. But let's not forget old favorites either, such as Gruyère scattered over a vegetable gratin, the salty bite of feta in a Greek salad, and cool, creamy buffalo's milk mozzarella with tomatoes and basil.

My passion for cheese has lasted throughout my career, and every time I discover a new variety I find it impossible to resist the urge to take it into the kitchen and experiment. I very much hope that reading this book will inspire you to do likewise.

how cheese is made

Cheese could be described as an inspired collaboration between Man and Nature. Part of my fascination with it stems from the astonishing diversity that is created out of a single product—milk. Consider the sheer scope and variety of the world's cheese. Then consider that they all are made from milk—many from cow's milk but some from the milk of goats, sheep, water buffalo, and even, in some remote areas, donkeys and horses.

The magical property of milk that enables us to turn it into cheese is its ability to curdle. This is said to have been discovered accidentally by Arab nomads many centuries ago, when a bag of ewe's milk was cut open to reveal a curd-like substance. The heat from the sun had turned the milk sour, causing it to coagulate. Nowadays, most cheese is made from milk that has been pasteurized, that is heated to 162°F for just 15 seconds and then cooled rapidly to 88°F. This destroys the bacteria that cause the milk to sour and curdle, so rennet has to be added to induce coagulation.

Pasteurization is a controversial subject, with many cheese connoisseurs believing that a great cheese can only be made from unpasteurized or "raw" milk, since this contains the bacteria that contribute to the cheese's flavor and character. On the other hand, food technologists will argue that pasteurized milk is "clean" milk. This may be the case in factory cheesemaking, where milk is collected in large tankers from a number of different suppliers, making it difficult to monitor the quality of the raw product. But artisan cheese is usually made from milk produced on the farm, giving the cheesemaker complete control over its quality.

The uniform character of pasteurized milk enables the cheesemaker to achieve a consistent product, which can reach a very high standard. But the truth is that the majority of great cheeses are made from unpasteurized milk, although there are some surprising exceptions to the rule, such as Colston Bassett Stilton.

Besides the type of milk used, many factors influence the character of each cheese, from the pasture, breed of animal, climate and even the time of year, to the way the curds are cut, the shaping, and the maturing process.

Once the milk has been soured, usually with a starter culture, rennet may be added and the milk clots into a fairly solid junket. This needs to be cut up to allow the whey to drain out. For softer cheeses, the curd is lightly cut and then left to drain naturally. For hard cheeses it is cut finely and then, in some cases such as for Parmesan, scalded, or "cooked," at 105-130°F so that it becomes dense and more whey can be drained off. The curd settles at the bottom of the vat, where it is milled again into small pieces.

Other than the softest cream and cottage cheeses, all chesses are salted with either dry salt or brine. Some soft and semi-soft varieties are also sprayed and washed with various solutions or with bacteria. Such measures encourage certain styles of ripening and the formation of particular types of rind.

The curd is ladled into suitable molds and pressed. Hard, compressed cheese is pressed heavily, while the curd may be left to firm naturally or only lightly pressed for most soft and semi-soft ripened cheeses.

Unripened cheese such as cottage cheese or fromage blanc are eaten fresh, but most cheeses go through a final stage of ripening, or maturing. This crucial process allows cheese to develop its character with time—from as little as four weeks for a Camembert to as much as four years for a Parmesan. During ripening, which takes place in a controlled atmosphere, the microbes and enzymes change their composition. Each stage contributes to the final character of the cheese and is carefully monitored by the cheesemaker.

choosing and storing cheese

Always try to buy cheese from a specialist merchant, who will give good advice and, usually, allow you to sample what's on offer. Go for farmhouse or artisan cheeses, which tend to be far more interesting in character and flavor than plastic-wrapped, factory-produced ones. Whenever practical, purchase whole cheeses or blocks of a decent size. Small portions can lose their flavor quickly.

Advice on storing individual types of cheese is given below, but there are a few general guidelines to bear in mind:

The ideal storage place is a cool pantry or cellar, about 50-60°F. This idyllic atmosphere neither retards the flavor nor hinders any ripening process. Nowadays, however, most people are resigned to storing cheese in the refrigerator. In this case, select the least cold part and aim for a temperature of 45-48°F.

If you do store cheese in the refrigerator, place each one in a separate airtight container. Certain varieties, notably the strong-smelling ones, are best wrapped in foil first. Avoid plastic wrap as it makes cheese sweat. Any cheese sold in its own box, Camembert for example, should be stored in the box. I never freeze cheese, as all too often this gives it a dry, grainy texture.

hard and semi-hard cheeses

Hard cheeses are ones that have been heavily pressed to give them a dense texture. The hardest include the extra-firm Italian grana cheeses, of which Parmigiano Reggiano, commonly known as Parmesan, is the most highly esteemed. Wonderful for grating, the grana cheeses also include grana pandana and pecorino Romano, which is made from sheep's milk.

At the softer end of the range are the semi-hard cheeses, which include Tilsit, Danbo, Samsow, Manchego, California's Monterey Jack, and Lancashire—of which the finest is probably Kirkham's Lancashire, one of my favorite cheeses.

Somewhere in the middle of the hard and semi-hard category is a huge grouping that includes three sub-groups: Cheddar-type cheeses, Gouda-type, and Gruyère-type.

Cheddar-type cheeses are cooked, pressed cheeses of middling firmness. They are prized all over the world for their sweet, full flavor and culinary adaptability. Hence it is possible to find Cheddars of English, American, Canadian, Australian, and New Zealand origin. France's equivalent is Cantal. However, the only true Cheddars are the great English farmhouse cheese, such as Montgomery's and Keen's from Somerset. Other cheeses related to this family are crumbly, piquant Cheshire (I am particularly fond of Appleby's Cheshire); very crumbly, mild Caerphilly, of which the supreme example is Duckett's Caerphilly; mellow Double Gloucester, orange-hued Leicester, and mottled-green Sage Derby, whose curds are infused with liquid sage extract.

Gouda-type cheeses are typically straw-colored with a thin rind and a coating of paraffin wax. Although Holland's authentic Gouda continues to be made in the town of that name near Amsterdam, other countries produce versions of it under an assortment of names—Teifi (Welsh), Broodkaas (Belgian), and German Gouda. Similar to Gouda is Edam, which is made of partially skimmed milk and therefore popular with those who count calories.

Gruyère-type cheeses range in flavor from a mellow nuttiness to a rich, full taste that is almost fruity and sweet. Their characteristic holes are formed by adding the popolonic acid bacterium. Swiss Gruyère has tiny pinprick holes spaced so far apart that they are sometimes difficult to see. Comté, Appenzell, and fontina have virtually no holes at all. The Norwegian cheese Jarlsberg has large holes, eclipsed only by the huge ones of Emmenthal.

Gruyère-type cheeses are invaluable in the kitchen. They grate cleanly and effortlessly, melt down rapidly and smoothly, and lend their fine, nutty flavor to a dish without overwhelming the other ingredients.

Choosing and Storing

Even the hardest of the grana cheeses should be moist. The rind and surface should not be cracked, neither should the surface show signs of sweating. Avoid Cheddar-types that are darker near the rind or at their cut edges, as this may indicate that they have dried out. Never buy pre-grated grana cheeses: no matter how fresh they claim to be, the flavor will deteriorate within hours.

Grana cheese such as Parmesan that you intend to use for grating will keep very well double-wrapped in foil in the refrigerator. Hard and semi-hard cheeses for the cheeseboard should, ideally, be stored in a cool pantry, with the cut surfaces covered by foil and the crust free to breathe. Failing that, store them as for grana cheeses for grating. They will keep well in the refrigerator for at least a week but no more than two. Bring them to room temperature before serving.

soft and semi-soft ripened cheeses

These have a high water content and undergo a similar ripening process to the above. Soft ripened cheeses contain 50-70 percent water, are spreadable, and include Brie, Camembert, Bonchester, and Pencarreg. Semi-soft ripened cheeses, such as Bel Paese, Gubbeen and Reblochon, contain 40-50 percent water and often feel springy to the touch.

Because they are moist and therefore more susceptible to microbes than hard cheeses, they ripen in a matter of weeks rather than months. Unlike hard cheeses, which are ripened from within by adding a starter bacteria to them, soft ripened cheeses are ripened from the outside, by the action of a surface mold which is sprayed on after salting. In order to create a bloomy white rind, such as the one on Brie, Camembert, and Coulommiers, the cheese is sprayed with the mold Penicillium candidum. The relatively mild, creamy characteristics of semi-soft cheeses such as Bel Paese and Morbier are achieved by washing the rind with a brine that slows down bacterial development.

Some semi-soft varieties, such as Port Salut, Münster and Reblochon, are known as monastery cheeses because they are ripened by a method developed by Trappist monks. The rind is washed with solutions that include alcohol—usually wine, beer or liqueur—resulting in a tangy flavor, savoury aroma and distinctive rind. Nowadays a culture of Breyibacterium linens might be used instead. This creates a thin, yellowish-red bacterial growth on the rind, which is not eaten.

Choosing and Storing

Soft ripened cheeses with white bloomy rinds should never smell of ammonia, nor should their rind show signs of hardness or browning. The paste should not ooze excessively. Ripe, whole cheeses should feel springy to the touch. The paste of cut wedges should look plump and even textured; a chalky line indicates underripeness.

Semi-soft ripened cheeses, including the monastery varieties, should possess a fruity—but never rank—aroma and feel slightly elastic. The rind should look fresh and ungummy.

soft fresh cheeses

pasta filata cheeses

Store soft and semi-soft ripened cheeses wrapped—or in the case of monastery cheeses doubled-wrapped—in foil in an airtight box in the refrigerator. The soft cheese Vacherin Mont d'Or is a case apart: it should never be refrigerated. You should keep it in a cool, damp place and press a block of wood against cut surfaces to prevent them running.

Bring soft ripened varieties to room temperature for two hours before serving. Once fully ripe they stay at their best for only a day or two. Semi-soft ripened cheeses such as Bel Paese keep for up to ten days, while the monastery cheeses vary in their keeping ability—from two to three days for Pont l'Évêque and up to a week for Reblochon.

These are uncooked and unripened cheeses. Uncooked means that the curds are not heated in their whey—which would encourage them to harden and cohere—while unripened indicated that the cheeses have not been ripened for more than a few days. They are too young to have developed any rind. Most soft fresh cheeses are made from cow's milk, often skimmed of its fat. Examples include cottage cheeses, curd cheese, fromage frais, fromage blanc, quark, pot or farmers cheese.

Fresh ricotta, one of the gems of Piedmont, is different. Traditionally it is prepared from the whey left over from sheep's milk after making pecorino. However, sometimes the whey from other cheeses, including cow's milk varieties is used. Ricotta's dry, bland texture makes it ideal for blending with other ingredients in both savoury and sweet dishes.

Cream cheese is, as the name implies, made from cream rather than milk. One of the most celebrated examples is mascarpone, which was originally made only in Lombardy in autumn and winter. It is created from cream that has been skimmed from whole milk. Once its curds have formed, they are drained for about 24 hours and then whipped to a texture like very thick double cream. Mascarpone tastes delicate and slightly sweet and has many culinary uses, its affinity with fruit and chocolate being surpassed only by its empathy with savoury ingredients.

Choosing and Storing

These cheeses should look and smell very fresh, clean and white, with no grubby edges. On no account should they ever taste bitter. Ricotta bought loose from a good Italian foodshop or cheese shop has an incomparable sweet, fresh flavor that bears no resemblance to the type sold in tubs. It must be eaten within a day or two, as the flavor becomes quickly tainted. All soft fresh cheeses are highly perishable. If possible, use a cool bag to carry them home and then put them on the coldest shelf of the fridge. Very moist types of ricotta, cottage, and curd cheese benefit from being stored in the refrigerator on a draining plate covered with a bowl. The drier fresh cheeses, including cream cheese, can be placed directly in an airtight container—lined with wax paper or foil. Use soft fresh cheese within four days.

Pasta filata is an Italian term meaning "spun paste" and refers to a technique of immersing the curd in hot water or whey, then kneading and stretching it. Well known Pasta filata cheeses include mozzarella, a semi-soft, unripened cheese made with the milk of cows or water buffalo; provolone, a ripened cheese that is available as a mild dolce or a stronger-tasting piccante; and Caciocavello, which is also ripened, often smoked, and can be just firm enough to slice when young or hard enough to grate when mature. All such cheeses are widely used in the Italian kitchen, especially for toppings, fillings and stuffings.

Choosing and Storing

If bought loose from an Italian grocer, mozzarella should have an immaculately white color and a fresh, lactic smell. Otherwise, buy the type sold in a little sachet of whey rather than the dry, plastic-wrapped ones. Buffalo's milk mozzarella is considered superior to cow's milk because of its stronger flavor and softer, less rubbery texture. Provolone should possess a faint, lactic aroma. With both provolone and Caciocavello, look for a fine glossy rind and avoid holes in the paste, as these may indicate internal fermentation.

Mozzarella bought loose should immediately be immersed in milk, left in the refrigerator and consumed within five days. With supermarket versions in their sealed bags of whey, honour the expiration date and keep any partially used portions in the whey in a dish. Store provolone and Caciocavello double-wrapped in foil. Provolone will keep well for one week in a cool place or the refrigerator and Caciocavello for up to two weeks.

goat cheeses

blue cheeses

Ranging in texture from soft and creamy to dry and sliceable, goat's milk cheeses are now made in countries all over the world. In France they are known as chèvre, the generic term for such cheeses. While they all share a dry, piquant aftertaste, their tangy- and unmistakably "goaty"—flavor varies in strength according to the region of production, altitude, ripening period, and mold cultures.

Traditionally produced on small farms or co-operatives throughout France and the Mediterranean, chèvre is made into a variety of small shapes: logs (bûches), dainty cylinders (bûchettes), little bells (clochettes) and an assortment of pyramids, disks, and so on. The name crottin—which, you may or may not wish to know, means horse droppings!—refers to the shape of the small, hard, round goat cheeses and also to their slightly darker coloring. Crottin de Chavignol is the best-known example and is highly prized for its bracingly sharp, full flavor.

In recent years goat cheeses have become very popular in Britain, Australia and the United States, with many small cheesemakers producing their own unique versions. Montrachet is possibly the best-known American variety, while Kervella is produced in Western Australia and Chabis, Golden Cross, Roubiliac, Tymsboro' and many others in Britain.

Choosing and Storing
Because there is such diversity and seasonal variance within this group, it is best to sample before you buy, That way you will be sure that the degree of tartness, ripeness, dryness, and so on is to your taste. Autumn and spring are partic-ularly good times to buy, although crottin de Chavignol tends to be better in winter. Avoid tough-looking rinds unless, of course, you want a well-aged crottin. Don't buy cheese with messy coloring or a rancid smell. Many goat cheeses are sold slightly underripe. Bear in mind that they will continue to mature and will ripen quickly if left beneath a cloche at a room temperature of, say 68°F. If you want to hold the cheese at a particular stage of maturity, wrap it in foil and store it in an airtight container in the fridge. Most goat cheeses will keep well in this way for at least a week.

Blue cheeses acquire their characteristic veining from mold spores. These may be introduced to the milk before it is soured and then encouraged to develop during ripening, when the cheese is pierced with fine needles. This allows the air in so the mold can spread.

The most noble blur cheese must surely be Roquefort. Some 2,000 years ago it acquired its veining from the natural Penicillium glaucum, which thrived in the limestone caves of the Combalou plateau in France. In 1411 Charles VI bestowed a royal charter upon these caves, thereby initiating the Roquefort appellation, or quality control, which still exists today. Unusually for a blue cheese, Roquefort is made with sheep's milk, which is partly responsible for its pungent flavor. In cookery, its assertiveness works wonderfully well with other robust ingredients.

Italy's champion blue cheese is Gorgonzola, which is milder, softer and less salty than Roquefort. Both cheeses have very little rind.

Britain's most illustrious example is Stilton, of which the finest is Colston Basset Stilton. It has a distinctive rind and is moist and creamy. More recent British blues include Dunsyre Blue (cow's milk) and Lanark Blue (sheep's milk) from Scotland, and Beenleigh Blue (sheep's milk) from Devon.

Ireland's most famous is Cashel Blue which, like Roquefort and Gorgonzola, has a foil-wrapped rind. Its particularly creamy texture blends smoothly in cooking. Other soft-textured blues that cook well include the American Oregon Blue and Maytag Blue.

Choosing and Storing
Choose Roquefort in its prime, that is from around six months old. In perfect condition it will have a creamy, moist, virtually white paste and a uniform greenish-blue veining. It should have just a faint smell of mold. These guidelines apply to most blue cheeses that are wrapped in foil, except their paste is not quite as ivory-white as that of Roquefort and some of them reach maturity at only three months.

Gorgonzola should be springy to the touch and never brownish and hard. Contrary to popular belief, it should not have a pungent smell. Stilton should be creamy-ivory, with an even distribution of greenish-blue veining. It should be open-textured and never dry, hard or salty.

Wrap all foil-finished blue cheeses except Gorgonzola in a double layer of foil and keep them in an airtight container in the refrigerator. Gorgonzola is better wrapped in a damp cloth and stored in a cool place. All these cheeses should stay in good condition for 8 to 12 days. Be sure to bring them back to room temperature before serving.

The best way to store Stilton is wrapped in a linen cloth in a cool cellar or pantry. Moisten the cloth if the cheese starts to dry out. If these conditions are impracticable, store it as for Roquefort.

the cheeseboard

The cheeseboard in a good restaurant will offer 10 to 15 varieties of cheese, chosen for their different characters and strengths. At home, it is better to have a small selection of cheeses in their prime than a large number in poor condition. A small selection is also less confusing to the palate, enabling your guests to relish each cheese to the full. It generally makes sense to offer one hard or semi-hard cheese, one semi-soft and one blue.

If possible, buy from a good cheese shop, where the cheeses are properly stored and staff will be able to advise you. As a change, it can be fun to put together an alternative cheeseboard—see pages 183-9 for ideas.

Bring refrigerated cheese to room temperature for at least an hour before serving to allow the full flavor to develop. However, the prepared cheeseboard should not be left in a warm room for more than 40 minutes, otherwise the cheeses may sweat. One way of overcoming this is to put the cheeses on the board and cover them with a damp cloth. I like only wooden boards, and I provide a separate knife for each cheese to prevent the different flavors from intermingling.

There is an art to cutting cheese so that the cheeseboard continues to look appetizing and wastage is minimized. Small square or round cheeses, such as Camembert, should be cut in half (diagonally if it is a square cheese) and then into small triangular wedges. It used to be considered bad manners to cut the "nose" off a wedge of brie, and it certainly leaves an unappe-tizing piece of rind. Instead, long slices should be taken from alternate sides so that it maintains its shape. Tall, thin pieces of cheese, such as a wedge from a whole Cheddar, can be laid on their side, making it easier to cut off long slices. Finally, truckles such as Stilton need to have a 'lid' cut off the top. You can then either slice off whole rounds or score a line round the cheese an inch or so from the top and cut down to give small wedges. Replace the lid when storing the cheese.

What to serve with cheese? I prefer something simple such as crusty bread and perhaps some tart grapes, crisp apples, or ripe pears. I avoid biscuits and butter since I am not convinced that they enhance the cheese. Occasionally, though, I do like to serve a good chutney with a farmhouse Cheddar or similar cheese (see pages 186-8).

how to taste cheese

When tasting cheese, consider these helpful guidelines:-

Before tasting, always allow the cheese to come to room temperature. This allows the aromas and flavors to be at their maximum potential.

Milder cheeses should be tasted first, then contintue with some stronger-flavored ones. Leave full-flavored blue-veined and pungent "stinky" cheese until last.

Ideally, you should taste each cheese at its center first, working your way to the outside, where the cheese will be the most aged and consequently the strongest in flavor.

I always start tasting from the tip of my tongue, working the cheese towards the back of the mouth. This way the cheese forms individual flavor characteristics as it comes into contact with the flavor sense areas, ie. sweet, salty, sour, hot, etc.

When tasting cheese, consider

Texture—smooth, grainy, supple

Density—how compact it feels in your mouth

Flavor—how flavorsome is the cheese, is it clean, cloying, mild, strong, fruity?

Acidity—is it lemony?

Finish—do the flavor characteristics linger in the mouth (similar to that of wine)?

Saltiness—is the cheese well-balanced?

Conclusion flavors—earthy, nutty, toasted, grassy, mushroomy, creamy, pungent, piquant

Aroma—smell the cheese, get a feel for its aroma, as you would with a wine

serving wine with cheese

Alain Senderens, the well-known Parisian chef-restaurateur, regards the partnership of cheese and wine as so important that he displays a list of famous cheese and wine marriages in his restaurant. Ultimately, however, personal taste should play a part—although a few general rules hold good, such as strong cheeses need a full-bodied wine, while mild ones are better matched with a light wine.

One common fallacy that I am happy to ignore is that all cheese goes with all red wine. This isn't the case. You must take into account the individual nature of both the cheese and the wine. Blanket statements about cheese and wine being good companions refer to everyday or indifferent wines. Certainly if a wine has negative qualities, these will be masked by cheese, especially a strong-flavored one. By the same token, a powerful cheese will overwhelm the exquisite subtleties of a fine wine.

That said, there are many magical partnerships that are very easy to get right, particularly if you are looking for a match for a decent red wine—perhaps one that has been carried over from the main course. In this case, you could choose from the many hard and semi-hard cheeses, such as Gruyère, Beaufort, Comté, Emmenthal, Appenzel, mild Cheddar, Cheshire, and fontina to name a few. You might also pick your way carefully around the semi-soft and soft cheeses, Among the soft fermented cheeses, Reblochon and Pont l'Évêque are probably the best bet, but only if they have been well cared for and remain delicate—almost sweet—in flavor. Be very cautious if you want to include Camembert and Brie; when ripe, these cheeses can acquire an acrid taste of ammonia that will kill good wine. It is best not to buy them too far in advance because they deteriorate rapidly after a day or two.

If you are serving a Sancerre or Pouilly Fumé with the main course and suspect it will be carried over to the cheese course, then you have the opportunity to enjoy one of the world's most sublime cheese and wine alliances, that of white goat cheese and flinty white wine. With a selection of at least six goat cheeses, you can create a cheeseboard that is visually very exciting, particularly if you line the board, or a large flat-bottomed basket, with glossy green grape leaves, or plane tree or chestnut leaves.

One of the great challenges of the cheeseboard is finding a match for strong, salty, blue cheese, whose aggressive nature has a distinctly discouraging effect on fine red wines. Roquefort, for example, despite its wondrous qualities, will completely annihilate most wines. However, most blue cheeses—and Roquefort in particular—make good partners for Sauternes and other dessert wines. So you can serve Sauternes with the dessert course, then continue the wine into the cheese course.

If you don't plan to offer a desert wine, port goes well with strong blues, especially Stilton. If you're particularly keen on having a red wine, you could try a powerful, full-bodied one such as Zinfandel or, for special occasions, Gigondas or Côte Rotie.

A young-to-middle-aged Gorgonzola or Bresse Bleu, or a milder blue such as dolcelatte or dolcelatte torta, is a good match for a Zinfandel, Barolo or Barbaresco. A well-aged Gorgonzola, however, would probably be too challenging in its pungency and sharpness even for such robust wines.

cooking with cheese

All cheeses have unique characteristics but there are a few points to bear in mind when deciding which to cook with. Generally I find I use fresh cheeses more in summer for light dishes and desserts and in winter harder cheeses, which add warmth and depth of flavor. Hard cheeses such as Parmesan, Cheddar, and Gruyère are the most popular for cooking. Their good melting qualities make them ideal for sauces, pasta, and gratins. Blue cheeses lend real depth of flavor to dishes, and pungent ones such as Roquefort should be added sparingly. Soft rinded cheeses such as Brie and Camembert types are not often used in cooking because their large proportion of rind makes them wasteful. However, they are delicious melted on top of soups or bread and can also be broiled or baked whole. Goat cheese are increasingly popular and are very versatile—try them in salads, pizzas, sauces, stuffings, and even desserts.

Cheese reacts differently depending on how it is cooked. The main principle is that it should not be exposed to too fierce a heat—except when broiling, in which case the cooking time should be brief. Overcooked cheese tends to be rubbery. Above a certain temperature the protein coagulates, separating the fat and water to produce a stringy texture. The secret is to add the cheese towards the end of cooking. If you are using it in a sauce, always take the pan off the heat and allow the cheese to melt in.

Hard cheeses can withstand higher temperatures than soft ones. Varieties such as haloumi, feta, and mozzarella are best cooked quickly at a high temperature. The classic example is mozzarella cooked in the blazing heat of a traditional pizza oven. The high fat or water content of soft cheeses means they blend easily with liquid, making them useful for vinaigrettes and other uncooked sauces (see the recipe for Goat Cheese and Cumin Vinaigrette on page 20).

Finally, a couple of tips: when grating cheese, chill it first to firm it up as this makes the job easier. And take care when seasoning cheese dishes as most cheeses contain added salt—taste first.

cheese and your health

Cheese can make a valuable contribution to our diet, supplying generous amounts of protein, vitamin A, and calcium, which helps prevent osteoporosis. It also contains vitamins B2, B12 and D, niacin and folic acid, as well as phosphorus and zinc. It is beneficial to children, because calcium aids the growth of strong bones and teeth, and also to the elderly, because it provides a concentration of nutrients that might otherwise be lacking in their diet. The vitamin B12 is especially welcome for vegetarians, who may like to seek out cheeses made with a vegetarian rennet substitute rather than traditional rennet—a substance extracted from the stomach lining of calves to clot the milk.

There's no denying, however, that many cheeses are high in fat—a cause of dietary concern for most of us nowadays. But I do believe it's possible to enjoy cheese as part of a healthy diet. As in all things, moderation is the key. Set out to discover the wealth of artisan cheeses on offer and enjoy them just two or three times a week. This is more satisfying than consuming bland, plastic-wrapped, factory-produced cheeses on a daily basis. A lump of good farmhouse cheese, a hunk of bread and some salad make for a fulfilling meal and you won't need butter or any other form of fat with it.

In cooking, it really pays to use good-quality cheeses. If you add a farmhouse Cheddar to your cheese sauce rather than a factory one, for example, you will find the taste is so much stronger that you can get away with using less. The farmhouse version may be more expensive but you will save on both calories and cost.

Soft ripened cheeses such as Brie and Camembert are not as calorific as you might think, containing around two-thirds the fat of hard cheeses such as Cheddar and only half the fat of Stilton. And, of course, there are cheeses that are naturally low-fat, mainly the soft ones such as ricotta, fromage frais, cottage cheese, and quark. You will find recipes for all of these in this book. But please, don't use the half-fat cheeses on sale in some supermarkets. These may have only half the fat but they have absolutely none of the flavor.

Several years ago, an irrational fear developed in Britain about the health risks of unpasteurized cheeses, which were wrongly seen as causing listeriosis. Since then, the government's Chief Medical Officer has completely exonerated unpasteurized cheeses, and, mercifully, they are just as safe to eat as pasteurized ones. However, there is a slight risk of listeriosis from rinded and mold-ripened cheeses (e.g. Camembert and Stilton), whether pasteurized or unpasteurized. Current advice is that these should be avoided by pregnant women, the very young, the very old, and anyone suffering from an immune-deficiency illness.

Typical Nutrition Values in Popular Cheeses Per 100g

Cheese	Carbs (g)	Fat (g)	Protein (g)	Calories (Kcal)
Brie	Trace	26.9	19.3	319
Camembert	Trace	23.7	20.9	297
Chaumes	1.0	25.4	21.0	317
Cheddar	0.1	34.4	25.5	410
Chèvre	Trace	25.6	21.0	314
Danish Blue	1.0	29.0	20.0	336
Dolcelatte	Trace	36.0	17.3	394
Edam	Trace	24.1	27.1	326
Feta	3.0	24.2	17.2	298
Fontina	0.1	30.45	25.2	381
Gorgonzola	Trace	26.0	19.0	333
Gouda	Trace	31.0	24.0	375
Gruyère	0.8	32.0	28.0	403
Mascarpone	4.8	40.30	5.5	404
Mozzarella (full-fat)	Trace	25.4	18.0	301
Mozzarella (half-fat)	1.8	10.5	20.0	182
Parmesan	Trace	32.7	39.4	452
Pont l'Évêque	Trace	22.5	24.0	299
Ricotta (full-fat)	2.6	14.8	10.0	185
Roquefort	1.8	29.0	21.0	352
Stilton	0.1	35.5	22.7	411

Notes on the Recipes

Butter is always unsalted.
Eggs are extra large free-range.
In white sauces, boiled milk is often specified. Although this is not essential, bringing the milk to a boil and then straining it before adding it to the sauce gives a smoother finish.

Alternative cheeses are suggested in most recipes. These are recommended replacements if the cheese in the ingredients list is hard to find, or Australian or American equivalents for readers in those countries. Occasionally, though, I have suggested a completely different cheese. This is to give a new twist to the existing recipe—for example, replacing the Cheddar in a soup with goat cheese or Stilton. Feel free to experiment.

IMPORTANT

Some of the recipes contain raw or lightly cooked eggs, which may carry a slight risk of salmonella poisoning. These should be avoided by the very young, the very old, anyone suffering from an immune-deficiency illness, and pregnant women.

Because of the marginal risk of listeriosis, it is also advisable that these groups steer clear of rinded and mold-ripened cheeses.

basics

There are as many different recipes for vegetable stock as there are cooks, but most of them contain sweet-tasting vegetables such as carrots and leeks.

vegetable stock

MAKES ABOUT 1 QUART

2 tablespoons olive oil
1 onion, chopped
1 small leek, chopped
1/2 cup chopped celery root
2 large carrots, chopped
1 celery stalk, chopped
3/4 cup chopped white cabbage
1/2 bulb fennel, chopped
4 garlic cloves, chopped
1/2 cup white wine (optional)
4 black peppercorns
1 sprig of fresh thyme
1 bay leaf
11/2 quarts water
2 teaspoons salt

Heat the oil in a large saucepan, add all the vegetables and the garlic and cook gently for about 5 minutes, until softened. Add the wine, if using, then add the peppercorns, thyme, bay leaf, and water.

Bring to a boil, add the salt and simmer for 40 minutes, until reduced by a third of its original volume. Strain through a fine sieve and leave to cool. Refrigerate until required or freeze.

PG TIPS

You can buy canned bouillion in supermarkets. These are generally of good quality and can be used in all the recipes requiring stock in this book. However, some of them are quite salty, so be careful when adding seasoning. Home-made stocks are, of course, considerably cheaper.

A light clear, refined chicken stock, ideal for sauces and soups.

chicken stock

MAKES ABOUT 71/2 CUPS

5 pounds raw chicken carcasses, or
    chicken wings and legs
21/2 cups chopped onions
11/2 cups chopped carrots
11/4 cups chopped celery
1 leek, chopped
1 bouquet garni (see Tip)

Put the chicken carcasses in a large pot, cover with cold water, and bring slowly to a boil. Skim off any impurities that rise to the surface, then add the vegetables and bouquet garni. Simmer very gently for 4 hours, then strain through a fine sieve and leave to cool. Refrigerate the stock until it is required or freeze.

PG TIPS

To make a bouquet garni, tie together 1 bay leaf and 2 sprigs each of fresh parsley and thyme and wrap in a small strip of green of leek.

This is ideal for using those last pieces of cheese and rind that are left after grating as much as you can from a piece. Parmesan is perfect for this recipe. The cheese adds a wonderfully rich flavor to the stock, which can be used as a base for risottos, pastas, sauces, and soups.

cheese-infused **chicken** stock

MAKES ABOUT 1 QUART

1 tablespoon unsalted butter
1 onion, sliced
1 leek, sliced
2 garlic cloves, halved
1 quart Chicken Stock
A few sprigs each of fresh parsley,
   rosemary & thyme
$1/2$ cup rinds of hard cheese

Heat the butter in a heavy-based pot, add the onion, leek, and garlic and cook over a gentle heat until softened. Add the chicken stock, herbs, and cheese rind and bring to a boil.

Reduce the heat and simmer for 20 minutes, then strain through a fine sieve and leave to cool. Refrigerate the stock until it is required or freeze.

You can use beef or veal bones to make this, but veal gives a better flavor.

meat stock

MAKES ABOUT 7$1/2$ CUPS

6 tablespoons vegetable oil
2 pounds beef or veal bones,
   chopped into small pieces
1 pound beef or veal trimmings,
   cut into small pieces
3 carrots, chopped
2 onions, chopped
1 celery stick, chopped
2 garlic cloves, crushed
$1/4$ cup tomato paste
1 bouquet garni (see Tip opposite)

Preheat the oven to 425°F. Heat half the oil in a roasting pan, add the bones and roast them for about 30 minutes, until well browned. Meanwhile, heat the remaining oil in a large pot and fry the meat trimmings until very well browned.

Add the bones, vegetables, and garlic to the pot, cover with water and bring slowly to a boil. Skim off any impurities that rise to the surface. Stir in the tomato paste and bouquet garni and simmer over a very low heat for 2 hours, skimming frequently. Strain through a fine sieve and leave to cool. Refrigerate until required or freeze.

reduced **meat** stock

Pour the strained meat stock into a pan and boil until reduced by half its volume. Store or freeze as above.

This is a classic white sauce that has been enriched with cream and egg and includes Gruyère cheese.

basic **cheese** sauce (sauce mornay)

MAKES ABOUT 2¹/₂ CUPS

3³/₄ cups milk
1 onion, peeled & studded with
 3–4 cloves
4 tablespoons unsalted butter
¹/₃ cup all-purpose flour
1 cup grated Gruyère cheese
1 teaspoon Dijon mustard
Freshly grated nutmeg
¹/₂ cup heavy cream
2 egg yolks
Salt & freshly ground black pepper

Alternative cheeses
For an interestingly different sauce,
replace the Gruyère with a goat
cheese or blue cheese

Put the milk and onion in a pan and bring to a boil, then remove from the heat and let stand for 5 minutes. Melt the butter in a separate pan and stir in the flour to make a roux. Cook gently, stirring, for 2–3 minutes.

Remove the onion from the milk and add the milk to the roux a little at a time, stirring constantly. Bring slowly to a boil, then reduce the heat and cook very gently for 20 minutes, stirring from time to time to prevent sticking.

Remove from the heat, add the cheese, and stir until melted. Add the mustard and season with nutmeg, salt and pepper. If you like, strain through a fine sieve for a smoother sauce. Stir in the cream and egg yolks.

This sauce is simple to make and the result is both satisfying and tasty.

rapid **cheese** sauce

SERVES 4

¹/₂ cup Vegetable Stock (see page 16)
¹/₂ cup heavy cream
6 tablespoons freshly
 grated Parmesan
2 teaspoons arrowroot
6 tablespoons chilled unsalted
 butter, cut into small pieces
Salt & freshly ground black pepper

Bring the vegetable stock and cream to a boil and boil for 2–3 minutes. Put the cheese and arrowroot in a bowl and mix to a paste with a little water. Add to the stock and stir over a gently heat until thickened. Whisk in the butter a few pieces at a time until smooth and creamy. Season to taste and serve immediately.

PG TIPS
To serve this sauce with fish, you can make it taste more interesting by adding fresh herbs such as chervil, chives, and tarragon.

These can be prepared well ahead of time and stored in the refrigerator or even the freezer. You can then cut off slices to use as required—perhaps as a topping for grilled fish, steak or vegetables.

cheese butters

SERVE 4

camembert butter

MAKES ABOUT 3/4 CUP

Camembert cheese, rind removed
9 tablespoons softened
  unsalted butter
Freshly ground black pepper

Process all the ingredients together in a blender or food processor, then scrape out on to a piece of foil. Shape into a log and roll up in the foil, then chill until required.

roquefort butter

MAKES 1 HEAPED CUP

4 ounces Roquefort cheese
10 tablespoons softened
  unsalted butter
1 tablespoon chopped fresh parsley

Prepare as for Camembert Butter.

roquefort & green peppercorn butter

Stir 1 tablespoon crushed green peppercorns into the Roquefort Butter.

ricotta, lemon thyme & garlic butter

MAKES 1 CUP

1/2 cup ricotta cheese
1/2 cup softened unsalted butter
1 garlic clove, minced
1 tablespoon fresh lemon thyme
  leaves

Prepare as for Camembert Butter.

Throughout this book you will discover the versatility of this sauce. It is wonderful with fresh pasta and can also be used as a stuffing for vegetables, fish, or chicken if you halve the amount of olive oil. You could also vary the herbs, replacing the cilantro with basil, for example, or with a combination of fresh herbs.

cilantro & **goat cheese** pesto

MAKES ABOUT 1¼ CUPS

1 garlic clove, crushed
1 cup fresh cilantro leaves
1 tablespoon pine nuts
²/₃ cup extra-virgin olive oil
2 tablespoons freshly grated
  Parmesan cheese
3 ounces (about scant ½ cup)
  soft mild goat cheese, such as
  Sainte-Maure, Golden Cross,
  Roubiliac, or Montrachet
¼ cup mascarpone
Salt & freshly ground black pepper

Put the garlic, cilantro, and pine nuts in a blender and blitz to a purée, gradually adding the olive oil. Add the cheeses and blend again until the mixture has a thick, saucelike consistency. Season with salt and pepper.

This unusual vinaigrette can be served with spring vegetable salads and is also delicious with Carpaccio of Beef (see page 48) as an alternative to the dolcelatte mustard dressing.

goat cheese & cumin vinaigrette

MAKES ABOUT 1¼ CUPS

4 ounces (about ½ cup) soft mild goat
  cheese, such as Montrachet
2 tablespoons hot water
2 tablespoons red wine vinegar
½ tablespoon ground cumin
1 tablespoon chopped fresh oregano
1 egg yolk
7 tablespoons vegetable oil or
  groundnut oil
Salt & freshly ground black pepper

Put the goat cheese in a bowl, pour on the hot water, and beat until smooth and creamy. Add the vinegar, cumin, oregano, if using, and egg yolk and whisk together until blended. Gradually whisk in the oil and then season to taste, being careful with the amount of salt you add as some goat cheeses have a rather salty flavor.

Quark is extremely low in fat and so is very useful for anyone trying to reduce their fat intake–for whom mayonnaise would usually be out of bounds because of all the oil it contains. Although this recipe includes a little olive oil for flavor, most of it is replaced by quark, resulting in a healthier, more delicate mayonnaise.

quark mayonnaise

SERVES 4

2 egg yolks
2 tablespoons red wine vinegar
4 tablespoons olive oil
1 cup low-fat quark
2 tablespoons water
Salt & freshly ground black pepper

Alternative Cheeses
Low-fat fromage blanc, ricotta, or
Farmer's cheese

Whisk the egg yolks and vinegar with a pinch of salt until creamy. Whisk in the oil a little at a time, as if making mayonnaise, to form a light emulsion. Blend the quark with the water and add to the egg mixture, then season to taste with salt and pepper.

To make cheese pastry, add ½ cup freshly grated Parmesan to the flour with the butter.

basic pie pastry

MAKES 1 POUND

1½ cups all-purpose flour
¾ cup chilled, unsalted butter,
  cut into small pieces
1 egg, beaten
A pinch of salt

Sift the flour on to a work surface or into a large bowl. Add the butter and blend together with your fingertips until it has a soft, sandy texture. Make a well in the center and add the beaten egg and salt. Gently mix together with your fingertips to form a smooth, even dough. Wrap in plastic wrap and chill for about 30 minutes or until required.

This rich pastry is suitable for most sweet tarts.

sweet pastry

MAKES 1½ POUNDS

2½ cups all-purpose flour
1 cup unsalted butter, cut into small
  pieces (at room temperature)
A pinch of salt
1 cup confectioners' sugar, sifted
Finely grated zest of ½ lemon
1 egg, beaten

Sift the flour on to a work surface and make a well in the center. Put the butter, salt, sugar, and lemon zest in the well and then add the egg. With your fingertips, gradually bring the flour into the center until all the ingredients come together to form a soft dough. Knead very lightly for 1 minute, until completely smooth, then form the dough into a ball. Wrap in plastic wrap and chill for 2 hours.

This quick and easy brioche is great for breakfast, but can also be used in both savory and sweet dishes, such as Warm Brioche of goat cheese with Mixed Leeks (see page 40) and Croque Mademoiselle (see page 178).

brioche

MAKES 12 BUNS OR 1 LOAF

1 cake (0.6 ounce) compressed
  fresh yeast
2 tablespoons milk
4 cups all-purpose flour
1 teaspoon salt
1$\frac{1}{2}$ tablespoons sugar
4 eggs
$\frac{1}{2}$ cup softened unsalted butter
1 egg beaten with 1 tablespoon milk,
  to glaze

Dissolve the yeast in the milk. Sift the flour, salt, and sugar on to a counter and make a well in the center. Beat the eggs with the yeast mixture, then pour them into the well in the flour. Gradually work the flour into the eggs with the heel of your hand until a soft dough is formed, then knead it for 2–3 minutes. Work in the softened butter, using the same method, and knead for about 10 minutes or until the dough has a smooth texture. It will feel slightly sticky to the touch. Cover with plastic wrap and let rest in the refrigerator for 30 minutes.

Shape the dough into 12 balls and place in buttered individual brioche molds or shape into a loaf and place in a loaf pan. Cover and let rise in a warm place for 30–40 minutes, until doubled in size. Preheat the oven to 400°F.

Brush the brioche with the beaten egg and milk mixture and bake until golden brown—about 20 minutes for brioche buns, 40 minutes for a loaf. Turn out on to a wire rack to cool.

This loaf (see photograph on page 189) is very quick as it needs only one rising. Although most recipes tell you to use warm water when making bread, I find cold water works perfectly well. In fact, it is probably safer, since if the water is too hot it may kill the yeast and prevent the loaf rising.

cheddar & onion loaf

MAKES 1 LOAF

1 heaped teaspoon fresh yeast
$\frac{1}{2}$ cup water
2 teaspoons vegetable oil
2$\frac{1}{2}$ cups all-purpose flour
A pinch of salt
A pinch of sugar
1 egg, beaten
$\frac{1}{4}$ cup finely diced onion
1$\frac{1}{2}$ cups grated aged farmhouse
  Cheddar cheese
$\frac{1}{4}$ cup freshly grated Parmesan

Put the yeast in a small bowl, add the water, and stir until the yeast has dissolved. Stir in the oil. Sift the flour, salt, and sugar into a bowl and make a well in the center. Pour in the yeast liquid and half the beaten egg and then stir in the flour to make a soft dough. Turn out on to a lightly floured work surface and knead for 8–10 minutes, until smooth and elastic. Let relax for about 2 minutes, until they are fully incorporated. Shape the dough into a loaf and place it in a greased 8$\frac{1}{2}$- by 4$\frac{1}{2}$- by 2$\frac{1}{2}$-inch loaf pan. Cover with a damp dishtowel and let rise in a warm place for about 1 hour, until doubled in size.

Preheat the oven to 425°F. Brush the top of the loaf with the remaining beaten egg and bake for 25–30 minutes, until the bread is golden brown and sounds hollow when turned out of the pan and tapped on the bottom. Turn out on to a wire rack to cool.

This is an excellent way of using up tiny bits of crumbled Stilton or other blue cheeses. It may seem extravagant to use it in bread, but as the flavor is strong you don't need very much. (See photograph on page 189.)

stilton bread

MAKES 2 LOAVES

1 1/2 cakes (0.9 ounce) compressed
   fresh yeast
1 1/4 cups water
2 teaspoons malt extract
2 teaspoons golden syrup
4 1/2 cups all-purpose flour
2 teaspoons salt
5 ounces Stilton cheese (about
   1 heaped cup), crumbled

Put the yeast in a small bowl, add a little of the water, and stir to dissolve. Stir in the malt extract and golden syrup. Sift the flour and salt into a bowl and make a well in the center. Pour in the yeast and the remaining water and then stir in the flour to make a soft dough. Turn out on to a lightly floured work surface and knead for 8–10 minutes, until smooth and elastic. Return to the cleaned bowl, cover with a damp dishtowel and let rise in a warm place for about 50 minutes, until doubled in size.

Punch down the dough and divide it in half. Roll out each piece into a rectangle about 8 by 12 inches. Sprinkle the Stilton evenly over the dough and roll up tightly. Place in 2 greased 8 1/2- by 4 1/2- by 2 1/2-inch loaf pans or shape into rounds and place on greased baking sheets. Cover with a damp dishtowel and leave in a warm place, until risen. Preheat the oven to 400°F.

Sprinkle the loaves with a little flour and bake for 35–40 minutes, until the bread is golden brown on top and sounds hollow when turned out and tapped on the bottom.

Brioche dough is spread with mozzarella, olives, and sun-dried tomatoes and then rolled up, producing a colorful spiral pattern when sliced. It's wonderful to take on picnics fresh from the oven.

italian picnic loaf

MAKES 1 LOAF

1 tablespoon olive oil
2 garlic cloves, minced
1 cup sun-dried tomatoes in oil,
   drained & finely chopped
2 tablespoons chopped black olives
1 quantity of Brioche dough (see
   opposite)
1 ball of cow's milk mozzarella, well
   drained & cut into 1/4 inch slices
Butter, for greasing
1 tablespoon freshly grated
   Parmesan cheese
A little milk, for brushing

Heat half the olive oil in a small pan, add the garlic and cook gently for about 1 minute, until softened but not browned. Stir in the sun-dried tomatoes and olives and cook for 1 minute longer, then let cool.

Roll out the brioche dough into a 10-inch square. Brush with the remaining olive oil, then arrange the mozzarella in overlapping slices over the top, starting 2 inces in from the edge of the dough. Sprinkle over the olive and tomato mixture, then roll up the brioche tightly like a jelly roll.

Lightly butter a 9- by 5- by 3-inch loaf tin and dust it with the grated Parmesan. Put the brioche roll in the pan, cover with a damp dishtowel and leave in a warm place for 25 minutes, until risen and puffy. Preheat the oven to 400°F. Brush the loaf with a little milk and then bake for 25 minutes, until it is golden brown on top and sounds hollow when turned out of the pan and tapped on the bottom. Serve warm.

chapter 1 **first courses**

My inclusion of cream cheese in this traditional Greek smoked fish purée would doubtless bring tears to the eyes of locals. I find it mellows and rounds the smoky flavor of the roe—try it and see what you think.

taramasalata with **cream cheese** on tapenade crostini

SERVES 4

3 slices of white bread,
  crusts removed
1 garlic clove, minced
4 ounces tarama (salted, dried
  gray mullet roe) or smoked
  cod's roe, skinned
6 tablespoons cream cheese
3 tablespoons lemon juice
6 tablespoons olive oil
2 tablespoons tapenade
8 slices of crusty French bread,
  about 1/2 inch thick
Salt & freshly ground black pepper

Soak the white bread in a little water, or, better still, milk, for 5 minutes. Squeeze out the excess moisture, then place the bread in a blender or food processor. Add the garlic, roe, and cream cheese and blitz to a smooth purée. Add the lemon juice and 4 tablespoons of the olive oil and blend again, then transfer to a bowl. Season to taste, then chill for at least 2 hours.

To serve, mix the tapenade with the remaining olive oil. Toast the French bread, spread it with the taramasalata, and drizzle over the tapenade.

PG TIPS
Jars of tapenade, a black olive and anchovy paste, are readily available in supermarkets and specialty food shops. I like to serve these crostini with pre-dinner drinks or with a tipple of Ouzo. And why not?

The vibrant colors of this dish are almost as enticing as its robust flavors. Although I usually serve it warm, it is also very good cold. Substitute oregano or basil for the parsley, if you like.

twice-roasted red peppers with **haloumi,** capers & olives

SERVES 4

4 large red sweet peppers
1/4 cup olive oil
2 garlic cloves, thinly sliced
2 tablespoons chopped fresh
    flat-leaf parsley
12 black olives, pitted & halved
2 tablespoons capers,
    rinsed & drained
8 slices of haloumi, cut 1/2 inch thick
Salt & freshly ground black pepper

For the dressing
2 tablespoons white wine vinegar
1/2 cup olive oil
1/4 teaspoon Dijon mustard
1/2 small red chili pepper, seeded &
    finely chopped

Alternative cheese
Feta

Preheat the oven to 400°F. Cut the peppers in half lengthwise, brush with a little of the olive oil, and season with salt and pepper. Bake for 1 hour or until tender. Remove from the oven and leave until cool enough to handle, then peel off the skin and cut the peppers lengthwise into strips 3/4 inch wide.

Lightly brush a gratin dish with olive oil. Put the pepper strips in it, sprinkle with the garlic, parsley, olives, and capers, and season with salt and pepper. Lay the haloumi cheese slices on top and drizzle over the remaining olive oil. Bake for 10–12 minutes, until the cheese is just starting to melt.

Meanwhile, whisk together all the ingredients for the dressing and season to taste. Remove the peppers from the oven and drizzle the dressing over. Serve warm, with herb-grilled crusty bread (see Tip below).

PG TIPS
To make herb-grilled crusty bread, brush slices of baguette with olive oil and sprinkle with chopped fresh herbs, then toast under the broiler until golden.

This is my version of the Greek dish ktipiti, which is usually a dip rather than a mousse. The saltiness of the feta cheese contrasts well with the peppery arugula.

feta & roasted pepper mousse with arugula & pine nuts

SERVES 4

1 large red sweet pepper
2/3 cup olive oil
8 ounces Greek feta cheese
1 cup strained plain yogurt
1 garlic clove, minced
3 gelatin leaves
1 tablespoon balsamic vinegar
A handful of young arugula leaves
1 tablespoon pine nuts
Salt & freshly ground black pepper

Preheat the oven to 400°F. Rub the pepper with 2 tablespoons of the olive oil, place on a baking sheet and bake for 40 minutes or until tender. Leave until cool enough to handle, then peel off the skin. Cut the pepper in half and remove the seeds. Put the pepper in a blender with the feta, yogurt, garlic, and 4 tablespoons of the olive oil and blitz to a fine purée.

Put the gelatin in a small pan, cover with about 3 tablespoons of water, and leave for 5 minutes to soften. Melt over a gentle heat until clear. Stir it thoroughly into the purée and strain the mixture through a fine sieve. Season to taste. Pour into 4 ramekin dishes or coffee cups. Chill for 1–2 hours, to set.

Whisk together the balsamic vinegar and the remaining olive oil to make a dressing and season to taste with salt and pepper. Unmold the mousses on to individual serving plates. Toss the arugula and pine nuts with the dressing and arrange them around the mousses.

Corniottes are little triangular pastries that can be filled with sweet or savory ingredients. Baked until crisp, they are a speciality of Burgundy, where they are served as a snack. If you don't have any Marc de Bourgogne, you could use kirsch instead.

emmenthal corniottes with marc de bourgogne

MAKES ABOUT 20

1 heaped cup fromage blanc or
  cream cheese
2/3 cup crème fraîche
2 tablespoons Marc de Bourgogne
1 3/4 cups grated Emmenthal
2 eggs, beaten
Freshly grated nutmeg
1 quantity of basic pie pastry (see
  page 21)
1 egg beaten with 2 tablespoons
  milk, to glaze
Salt & freshly ground black pepper

Alternative cheeses
Swiss Appenzell or Gruyère

Preheat the oven to 400°F. Put the fromage blanc or cream cheese, crème fraîche, and Marc de Bourgogne in a bowl and beat in the grated Emmenthal and eggs to form a paste. Season with nutmeg, salt, and pepper and set aside.

Roll out the pastry until it is 1/4 inch thick and cut out 4-inch rounds—you should have about 20. Put some filling in the center of each one. Brush the edges with a little cold water and then pull 3 sides of the pastry up over the filling to form a point. Pinch together firmly to seal. Chill for up to 1 hour, then brush with the beaten egg and milk mixture and bake for 20–25 minutes, until golden. Serve hot or warm.

PG TIPS
Smaller corniottes make great cocktail canapés. They also freeze successfully, so they can be prepared in advance and baked straight from the freezer when required. Puff pastry works just as well as this pie pastry.

I love the textures of this warm smoked salmon and blue cheese salad, the salmon delicate and meltingly tender, while the creamy mild-tasting Cornish blue is an excellent contrast to the dressing.

seared smoked salmon & **cornish blue** salad

SERVES 4

7 ounces mixed salad leaves
1 medium carrot, finely shredded
6 ounces cherry tomatoes, halved
4 tablespoons French dressing
 (of your choice)
$2/3$ cup crumbled Cornish blue cheese
2 tablespoons mild olive oil
1 pound cleaned smoked salmon,
 cut into $1/2$-inch thick slices
2 cooked beetroots, cut into wedges
Small handful of fresh mint leaves
Salt & freshly ground black pepper

Place the salad leaves, carrot, tomato, and 3 tablespoons of the dressing in a bowl and toss together. Add half the Cornish blue cheese and season to taste. Divide the salad between 4 individual serving dishes.

Heat the oil in a nonstick frying pan, and when hot add the smoked salmon slices and quickly flash-fry for 10 seconds on each side, then remove and keep warm until you are ready to serve.

Divide the salmon between the 4 dishes and add the beetroot wedges. Sprinkle over the remaining cheese, drizzle with the remaining dressing, and scatter with mint leaves. Serve immediately.

The combination of oysters and blue cheese may sound unexpected but it is a marriage made in culinary heaven. This is my version of a dish I came across at the Bel-Air Hotel in Los Angeles, during a week I spent there as guest chef. The original recipe used Maytag Blue, a creamy, salty cheese from Iowa, but I have substituted Bleu d'Auvergne.

glazed oysters on crushed potatoes with parsley & **bleu d'auvergne**

SERVES 4

8–9 ounces new potatoes
1/4 cup milk
1/4 cup olive oil
2 tablespoons chopped fresh flat-
   leaf parsley
24 plump oysters
Salt & freshly ground black pepper

For the sauce
2 egg yolks
4 tablespoons dry white wine
2/3 cup heavy cream
1/2 cup crumbled Bleu d'Auvergne

Alternative cheeses
**Roquefort, Maytag Blue or
   Oregon Blue or Bellingham
   Blue (IRE)**

Cook the potatoes in boiling salted water until just tender, then drain well. Place in a bowl, add the milk, olive oil and parsley and crush them coarsely with a fork. Season with salt and pepper and keep warm.

Open the oysters and remove from the shells, reserving the juices (see Tip below). Discard the top part of each shell and clean the bottom part.

For the sauce, whisk the egg yolks and wine together in a small bowl, or the top of a double boiler. Set the bowl over a pan of simmering water and whisk until the mixture thickens and doubles in volume. Boil the cream and cheese together for 2–3 minutes, then fold into the whisked egg yolk and wine mixture along with the strained oyster juices.

To serve, divide the crushed potatoes between the cleaned oyster shells. Season the oysters, put them on top of the potato mixture, and coat with the sauce. Place under the broiler for 5 minutes, until golden (or place in a hot oven). Serve immediately.

PG TIPS
To open oysters you need an oyster knife or other short, strong-bladed knife.

Wrap your hand in a dishtowel to protect it, then take hold of an oyster and insert the knife blade between the shells, next to the hinge. Twist the knife to lever open the top shell, then cut the muscle connecting the oyster to the shell. Next, loosen the muscle connecting the oyster to the bottom shell. Take out the oyster and strain the juices into a bowl.

This simple recipe is a savory version of French toast. A good aged Taleggio cheese adds a creamy, aromatic, and slightly sour flavor, which partners the sweetness of the tomatoes and brioche well. If yellow plum tomatoes are available, why not use half red, half yellow? The colors look stunning.

parmesan brioche toast with **taleggio**, sautéed plum tomatoes, & oregano

SERVES 4

2 tablespoons olive oil
2 garlic cloves, crushed
1 pound small plum tomatoes, halved
2 tablespoons chopped fresh oregano
2 eggs, beaten
1/2 cup milk
1/2 cup freshly grated Parmesan cheese
Freshly grated nutmeg
4 slices of brioche (see page 22), cut 3/4 inch thick
3 tablespoons unsalted butter
1/2 cup aged Taleggio slivers
Salt & freshly ground black pepper

Alternative cheeses
Substitute freshly shaved Parmesan or Asiago for the Taleggio

Heat the oil in a pan, add the garlic, and cook for 1 minute. Add the tomatoes and sauté them until they begin to soften. Season with salt and pepper and stir in the oregano. Keep warm.

In a shallow bowl, whisk together the eggs, milk, and Parmesan cheese, seasoning with a little nutmeg, salt and pepper. Cut the brioche slices into rounds, if desired, or leave them whole. Dip them in the egg mixture on both sides. Heat the butter in a frying pan, add the brioche and cook for 2–3 minutes on each side, until golden.

Put the Parmesan French toasts on serving plates and arrange the tomatoes on top. Scatter over the Taleggio and place under the broiler to melt the cheese slightly before serving.

PG TIPS
It's important to use good, sweet, ripe tomatoes here. Plum tomatoes are generally fuller flavored, but if they are not readily available, try using the larger, rounded varieties, sliced. Add a pinch of sugar if their flavor is not all it should be. English muffins can be substituted for the brioche.

Although buffalo mozzarella is generally held to be superior to cow's milk mozzarella, in this recipe I actually prefer to use the cow's milk cheese because it is less milky in texture and holds its shape better.

ratatouille-stuffed **mozzarella** wrapped in prosciutto

SERVES 4

3 tablespoons extra-virgin olive oil
1 small eggplant, sliced
1 zucchini, sliced
1 garlic clove, crushed
1 teaspoon chopped fresh thyme
2 balls of cow's milk mozzarella
2 plum tomatoes, skinned & sliced
8 thin slices of prosciutto
4 tablespoons unsalted butter
Salt & freshly ground black pepper

For the dressing
2 tablespoons balsamic vinegar
6 tablespoons extra-virgin olive
  oil
1 tomato, skinned, deseeded & diced
1/2 tablespoon chopped black olives
6 fresh basil leaves, shredded

Alternative cheese
Provolone

To make the ratatouille, heat the oil in a frying pan and fry the eggplant and zucchini slices until tender. Stir in the garlic and thyme and cook for 1 minute, then season and leave to cool.

Cut each mozzarella horizontally into 4 equal slices and season lightly. Cover 4 slices with layers of eggplant, zucchini, and tomato, then top with the remaining cheese slices, making 4 ratatouille-stuffed mozzarella sandwiches in all. Wrap each one in 2 slices of prosciutto to secure the filling and chill for at least 30 minutes.

Heat the butter in a large frying pan, add the cheese sandwiches, and fry until golden, about 2–3 minutes on each side. Place on 4 serving plates. Mix together all the ingredients for the dressing and season to taste. Pour it over the cheese sandwiches and serve straight away.

PG TIPS
Try grilling the stuffed mozzarella over charcoal for a superb smoky flavor. Some people may be surprised to see that I do not advise salting the eggplant in this recipe. When slicing eggplant thinly, I really see little point in the exercise. However, when I use them in halves, I do usually salt them before cooking.

Moutabel is a Middle Eastern dish of puréed eggplant and tahini, also known as baba ghanoush. I find eggplants have a great affinity with cheese. In this dish, eggplant halves are stuffed with a moutabel-style filling and then topped with goat cheese and thyme. Serve on salad leaves with a dressing of Middle Eastern flavors, such as a vinaigrette containing peeled, deseeded and finely diced tomato, chopped cilantro and a little ground cumin.

roasted eggplant moutabel with **roubiliac** & thyme

SERVES 4

3 medium eggplants
2 tablespoons tahini
1 garlic clove, minced
1 teaspoon ground cumin
2 tablespoons lemon juice
1 Roubiliac goat cheese log, cut
 into 12 slices
2 tablespoons fresh thyme leaves
1/4 cup walnut oil
Salt & freshly ground black pepper

Alternative cheese
Any soft fresh goat cheese like
Coachfarm Goat or St Tola (IRE)

Preheat the oven to 375°F. Cut the eggplants in half, score the cut sides with a knife in a criss-cross pattern, and bake for 45 minutes to 1 hour, until tender. The exterior should be slightly charred but not burnt. Remove from the oven and let cool, then scoop out the flesh without damaging the skins. Mince the flesh and mix it with the tahini, garlic, cumin, lemon juice, and some salt and pepper.

Refill the eggplant skins with this mixture (there may only be enough to fill 4 halves), retaining the original shape of the eggplants. Put them in a lightly oiled, shallow baking dish. Top each one with the slices of goat cheese, sprinkle with the thyme leaves, and drizzle the walnut oil over. Return to the oven to bake for 8–10 minutes, until the cheese is golden and just beginning to melt. Cool slightly before serving.

This dish of simply fried sheep's milk cheese is served as a staple in tavernas throughout the Greek islands. Its beauty lies in its simplicity. It must be one of the easiest dishes to prepare, with just three ingredients, but it is delicious—and exceedingly more-ish.

saganaki (fried sheep cheese with lemon)

SERVES 4

6 tablespoons unsalted butter
8 slices of kasseri/kefalotiri cheese,
 3/4 inch thick
Juice of 3/4 lemon
Salt & freshly ground black pepper

Alternative cheese
Haloumi

Heat the butter in a large frying pan until foaming, add the cheese slices and fry for 1–2 minutes on each side, until golden. Season lightly with salt and pepper and then pour the lemon juice over the cheese in the pan. Serve right away, with lots of crusty bread.

PG TIPS
The lemon juice nicely flavors the butter; but to add an extra dimension I occasionally like to add fresh capers and herbs. In Greece, the cheese is sometimes flamed with brandy at the table.

Like flamiche (see page 41), goyère is a rich cheese tart from Belgium and northern France. Some recipes specify a pastry base while others use a bread dough, similar to that of a pizza. Here I give my favorite version, which has a yeasted dough for the base. The filling for goyère is generally made with a pungent—or, frankly, smelly—rindwashed cheese such as Maroilles or Livarot. Not for the faint-hearted, but when mixed with smoked bacon and potatoes it makes a wonderfully flavored dish.

goyère

SERVES 4–6

3 cups potatoes, cut into small cubes
2 tablespoons unsalted butter
1 small onion, minced
4 ounces (4 slices) bacon, chopped
4 1/2 ounces Munster cheese, rind removed, cut in 1/4 inch cubes (about 1/2 heaped cup)
2 eggs, beaten
1/2 cup crème fraîche or heavy cream
Salt & freshly ground black pepper

For the base
6 tablespoons unsalted butter
3 tablespoons milk
1 cake (0.6 ounce) compressed fresh yeast
2 cups all-purpose flour
2 eggs, beaten
A pinch of salt
A pinch of brown sugar

Alternative cheese
Connoisseurs should look out for an interesting English cheese called Stinking Bishop. The rind is washed with the pear variety of the same name, also used to make perry or pear cider, which gives the cheese its strong-smelling yet creamy-tasting character

For the base, warm the butter and milk over a low heat until the butter has just melted. Leave until tepid, then stir in the yeast until dissolved. Sift the flour into a bowl, make a well in the center and add the beaten eggs, salt, and brown sugar. Add the yeast mixture to the eggs and mix in the flour to give a smooth dough. Turn the dough out on to a lightly floured work surface and knead for 5 minutes or until smooth. Return it to the cleaned bowl, cover with a damp cloth, and let rise in a warm place until doubled in size.

For the filling, cook the potatoes in boiling salted water until just tender, then drain well. Heat the butter in a pan, add the onion, and cook over a gentle heat until soft but not colored. Add the bacon and cook for 5 minutes, then remove from the heat and set aside to cool.

Put the potatoes, onion, bacon, and cheese in a bowl and mix in the eggs and crème fraîche or cream. Season to taste with salt and pepper.

Punch down the risen dough and roll out until it is 1/4 inch thick. Use to line a 9-inch flan ring, leaving a good amount of dough overlapping the edge. Set on a baking sheet or a tart pan, fill with the potato, bacon, and cheese mixture and let rise in a warm place for 30 minutes, until the dough is puffy. Preheat the oven to 325°F.

Trim off the excess dough, then bake the tart in the oven for 45 minutes to 1 hour, until golden and set.

Ripe, sweet pears make an excellent foil for the sharp blue cheese and aromatic rosemary. As an alternative dish, try replacing the pear and Beenleigh Blue with slices of mozzarella and tomato, top them with a covering of pesto and bake the galettes as usual.

pear, **beenleigh blue** & rosemary galettes

SERVES 4

2 small egg whites
8–9 ounces Beenleigh Blue
1 tablespoon crème fraîche
1 quantity of shortcrust pastry
  (see page 21)
1 tablespoon finely chopped
  fresh rosemary, plus a few
  leaves to garnish
4 tablespoons unsalted butter, plus
  a little melted butter for brushing
2 large, ripe but firm pears, peeled,
  cored & cut into slices 1cm thick
1 tablespoon caster sugar
1 teaspoon cumin seeds
2 egg yolks, beaten with
  1 tablespoon milk, to glaze
Salt & freshly ground black pepper

Alternative cheeses
**A fairly sharp blue cheese is needed,
such as Gorgonzola, Roquefort,
Buxton Blue or Oxford Blue**

Whisk the egg whites until just frothy. Put the cheese in a bowl and crush it lightly with a fork, then add the egg whites and crème fraîche and mix to a coarse paste. Season with salt and pepper, then chill.

Roll out the pastry to about $1/8$ inch thick. Using a plain or fluted cutter, cut out four 5-inch discs. Put them on a baking sheet and prick well all over with a fork to prevent them rising too much in the oven. Carefully spread the cheese mixture over the pastry discs, leaving a $1/2$–$3/4$ inch border, then sprinkle with the chopped rosemary and place in the refrigerator.

Preheat the oven to 400°F. Melt the butter in a shallow pan, then add the pear slices, sugar and enough water to form a light syrup around the pears—about 3 tablespoons. Cook gently for 6–8 minutes, until the pears are tender, then set aside to cool.

Arrange the pear slices on top of the galettes in neatly overlapping circles and brush with a little melted butter. Sprinkle with the cumin seeds and a few rosemary leaves and season with salt and pepper. Bring up the edges of the pastry over the pears to form a crust. Brush the pastry all over with the egg yolk glaze and bake for 15–20 minutes or until golden. Cool the galettes slightly before serving.

PG TIPS
The galettes can be assembled several hours in advance—or even the night before—and chilled until you are ready to bake them. If you prefer, you can use puff pastry for the instead of the basic pie pastry.

I first prepared this brioche for a private party of eight vegetarians in the Lanesborough's Conservatory restaurant, as part of a seven-course gastronomic vegetarian menu. It was voted the star of the show and now makes regular appearances on my menu.

warm brioche of **goat cheese** with minted leeks

SERVES 4

4 tablespoons unsalted butter
2 young leeks, thinly sliced
1 tablespoon chopped fresh mint
Freshly grated nutmeg
4 brioche buns, 2 inches in diameter
  (see page 22)
4 crottin de Chavignol goat
  cheeses, cut horizontally in half
Salt & freshly ground black pepper

Alternative cheeses
A good English alternative is a well-aged Chabis, produced in East Sussex on the same farm as Golden Cross. Or you could use 4 slices of Sainte-Maure goat cheese, cut 1 inch thick

Preheat the oven to 400°F. Melt the butter in a pan, add the leeks and cook over a low heat for 8–10 minutes or until tender. You may need to add a little water if the leeks become too dry and stick to the pan. Remove from the pan and stir in the mint, then season to taste with nutmeg, salt, and pepper.

Cut a ½ inch slice off the top of each brioche and set aside, then carefully hollow out the center of each bun. Fill with the minted leeks. Top the leeks with the goat cheese and then put the brioches in the oven for 5 minutes to heat through. The cheese should just be starting to melt. Replace the brioche tops and serve immediately.

PG TIPS
Try topping the cheese with a little basil pesto before putting the brioches in the oven. I much prefer to prepare fresh pesto, which can be made in minutes in a blender. Store-bought pesto is fine, but nothing quite matches the flavor and aroma of fresh basil. Phyllo pastry makes a good substitute for the brioche. Simply top the leeks with the cheese and wrap well in the phyllo, then bake until golden.

Here's a Norwegian take on the Mexican dish. It makes a great appetizer or hearty snack. Serve with fresh tomato salsa and plenty of sour cream.

mediterranean tortillas with **jarlsberg**

SERVES 4

4 tablespoons olive oil

1 small eggplant, trimmed and thinly sliced

1 red sweet pepper, halved, seeded, and cut into strips 1cm wide

3 cups sunblush tomatoes in oil, drained

1 red chili, halved, seeded, and finely chopped

3 tablespoons fresh cilantro, roughly chopped

8 ounces Jarlsberg, freshly grated

8 large tortillas

1/2 cup tomato salsa

1/2 cup sour cream

Heat a large frying pan and add 3 tablespoons of oil. Add the eggplant, pepper, tomatoes, and chilli and stir-fry for 8-10 minutes, until tender. Remove from the heat. Add the cilantro and cheese and let it melt.

Lightly grease another frying pan with the remaining oil. Lay a tortilla flat in the pan and top with a quarter of the vegetables and cheese mix. Top with the second tortilla and press down gently. Cook over a medium heat until the bottom of the tortilla is golden and crisp—about 2 minutes.

Cover with a plate and turn the pan over to lift out the tortilla. Slide it back into the pan and brown the other side. Repeat with the remaining tortillas and filling. Cut into triangles and serve immediately with tomato salsa and sour cream.

I got the idea for this recipe from Pierre Carrier, the proprietor of the Hotel Albert Premier in Chamonix, France. His version used a local Reblochon made of goat's milk, which is well worth buying if you ever happen to see it. Although the dish is fairly expensive to make, the flavors are out of this world. Serve as a substantial first course or a delicious and unusual lunch dish.

baked **reblochon** in savoy cabbage

SERVES 4

3 tablespoons vegetable oil
2/3 cup potatoes, cut into
   1/4 inch cubes
1 onion, minced
3 ounces (3 slices) bacon, cut into
   lardons (small strips)
1 cup thinly sliced chanterelle
   mushrooms
1 1/2 cups thinly sliced button
   mushrooms
2 tablespoons chopped fresh chives
8 green cabbage leaves, such as
   Savoy or Primo
Freshly grated nutmeg
1 Reblochon cheese, rind removed
2 tablespoons unsalted butter,
   melted
1 1/4 cups Reduced Meat Stock
   (see page 17)
Salt & freshly ground black pepper

Alternative cheeses
Baby Saint-Nectaire, Pont-l'Évêque,
a plain or smoked Gubbeen,
Polkobin (AUS) or Jindi Brie (AUS)

Heat 1 tablespoon of the oil in a frying pan and sauté the potatoes until golden brown and just tender. Remove from the pan and set aside. Add the remaining oil to the pan and stir in the onion, and both types of mushroom. Raise the heat and cook until golden and tender. Add to the potatoes, stir in the chives and let cool.

Preheat the oven to 400°F. Trim the cabbage leaves and cook them in boiling salted water until just tender. Remove with a slotted spoon and refresh in cold running water, then drain well and dry on a cloth. Lay out the leaves, slightly overlapping, on a work surface and season with nutmeg, salt, and pepper.

Slice the Reblochon in half horizontally, cover one half with the potato mixture and top with the other half to form a sandwich. Place the Reblochon in the center of the cabbage leaves and fold them over to cover the cheese completely. Season again and brush with the melted butter. Place in a baking dish and bake for about 12–15 minutes, until thoroughly heated through. Meanwhile, heat the reduced meat stock. When ready, transfer the cheese to a serving dish and pour the meat stock around it. Serve cut into wedges.

PG TIPS
Try wrapping the cheese in puff pastry rather than cabbage leaves. Swiss chard or spinach could easily replace the cabbage, if preferred. For vegetarians, the meat stock can be substituted with red wine vinegar or walnut oil dressing.

You need kasseri cheese for this recipe, a mild, creamy sheep's milk cheese which is now available from some Greek grocers. The artichokes are filled with a tangy cheese and herb mixture, which also makes a very good stuffing for tomatoes and eggplants.

greek-style baked artichokes with cilantro, mint & lemon

SERVES 4

8 medium or 4 large globe
  artichokes
Juice & grated zest of 1 lemon
1 cup fresh white breadcrumbs
2 garlic cloves, minced
1 tablespoon chopped fresh mint
1 tablespoon chopped fresh
  cilantro
1/2 cup grated kasseri cheese
2/3 cup olive oil
3/4 cup crumbled feta cheese
2/3 cup dry white wine
Salt & freshly ground black pepper

Alternative cheeses
There is an American version of kasseri from Wisconsin, made with cow's milk and tasting a little sharper and saltier. Italian provolone could be used instead

Preheat the oven to 350°F. To prepare the artichokes, snap off the stalks and trim away the dark, fibrous outer leaves until you reach the tender, inner green leaves, rubbing the artichokes with the lemon juice as you go to prevent discoloration. Slice off about one third from the top of each artichoke. Carefully remove the hairy inner choke with a teaspoon. Drop the artichokes into a bowl of water acidulated with lemon juice.

In a bowl, mix together the lemon zest, breadcrumbs, garlic, mint, cilantro, grated kasseri, and 2 tablespoons of the olive oil. Season with salt and pepper.

Drain and dry the artichokes, then fill them with the feta. Top with the stuffing mixture. Place them in a baking dish, sprinkle over the white wine and the remaining oil and add water until the liquid reaches halfway up the sides of the artichokes. Bake for 35 minutes or until tender, basting frequently, then put the artichokes under the broiler for a few minutes to brown the stuffing. Serve hot or cold.

My good friend Stuart Partridge, chef at the Hassler Hotel in Rome, first prepared this dish during a recent visit to the Lanesborough. I love the pure simplicity of its flavors. You could serve the zucchini with a tomato sauce but I like them best with just a squeeze of lemon juice. Although very young, zucchini with their yellow flowers still attached are sold in markets in France and Italy, they are not as easily available in the US. However, if you grow your own zucchini or other summer squash, you can pick them for this recipe when they are just the right size.

crisp, flowering zucchini with **mozzarella** & anchovy

SERVES 4

8 zucchini, about 2 inches long,
  with flowers still attached
4 canned anchovy fillets
1 ball of cow's milk mozzarella
3 tablespoons Chinese flour
  (see Tip)
Vegetable oil for deep-frying
Salt & freshly ground black pepper
Sprigs of fresh flat-leaf parsley, to
  garnish
Lemon wedges, to serve

Trim about $1/2$ inch off the end of each zucchini and discard (or save for another use). Carefully wipe clean the zucchini flowers and remove the stamen from the center of each one. Soak the anchovy fillets in water for 10 minutes, then dry them on paper towels. Cut each anchovy fillet in half. Cut the mozzarella into 8 sticks approximately the size of your index finger. Place a piece of anchovy on each mozzarella stick, then place inside a zucchini flower and twist the end of the blossom to secure the filling. Repeat with the rest.

Mix the Chinese flour with enough water to make a thin batter; it should coat the back of a spoon. Heat the oil in a deep fryer or large saucepan to 350°F. Dip the stuffed zucchini in the batter and deep-fry them for 1–2 minutes, until crisp and golden, turning them occasionally. Drain them thoroughly on paper towels. Quickly drop the sprigs of parsley into the hot oil and fry for about 10 seconds, until crisp, then drain on paper towels. Serve the zucchini immediately, garnished with the deep-fried parsley and accompanied by lemon wedges.

PG TIPS

Chinese flour is available in Asian markets, but if you can't find any, make a tempura batter instead. Put 1 small egg yolk and $3/4$ cup iced water in a bowl, then gently mix in $2/3$ cup all-purpose flour and a pinch of salt; it should be slightly lumpy. Dip the stuffed zucchini in the batter and try as above. If you are keen to try this recipe but can't track down zucchini flowers, wrap the cheese and anchovy in blanched spinach or roll in sautéed thin slices of eggplant before frying.

This savory French toast is made with Emmenthal one of the great classic chesses. It is one of my favorite dishes for a real breakfast treat or light brunch option.

emmenthal "french toast" with asparagus & poached egg

SERVES 4

4 tablespoons unsalted butter
2 tablespoons chopped fresh chives
8 slices of good quality white bread, crusts removed
5 ounces Emmenthal cheese, thinly sliced
2 eggs, beaten
4 tablespoons milk
2 tablespoons freshly grated Parmesan
2 tablespoons double, whipping cream
Freshly grated nutmeg
2 tablespoons olive oil
1 tablespoon white wine vinegar
4 eggs
8 tender, green aspaprgus tips, peeled
Salt & freshly ground black pepper

In a bowl, cream 2 tablespoons butter with the chopped chives and a little salt and pepper. Butter all the slices of the bread on one side, then place Emmenthal cheese on 4 of them. Top with the remaining buttered slices to make 4 sandwiches.

In a bowl, whisk together the eggs, milk, cream, and parmesan, salt, pepper and a little pinch of nutmeg. Pass the 4 sandwiches through the egg mixture, making sure the mixture is soaked into the bread.

Meanwhile, heat a large nonstick pan and add the olive oil. When it is moderately hot, add a sandwich to the pan. Cook for 1–2 minutes on each side, until golden. Repeat with the other 3 sandwiches. You can do this in one motion so that you soak each sandwich, then transfer it to the pan, one at a time.

Meanwhile, bring 2 separate pans of water to a boil, add the vinegar to one pan and reduce to a simmer. Carefully crack the eggs into the pan and poach for 2–3 minutes until set, but still soft in the center. (You may have to do this in two gos.) Remove and drain the eggs on a dishcloth and some paper towels. Cook the asparagus tips in the other boiling water. Remove and drain, season with salt and pepper, and finish with the remaining butter.

To serve, cut the French toasts in half diagonally, place 2 French toast halves on each serving plate. Top with the asparagus tips and a poached egg. Serve immediately.

This mustard and blue cheese dressing makes a good alternative to the olive oil and Parmesan cheese that normally accompany carpaccio of beef. To make a warm carpaccio, use thin steaks—about 1/4 inch thick—and grill over charcoal for about 1 minute per side.

carpaccio of beef with **dolcelatte** mustard dressing

SERVES 4

1 pound beef tenderloin
1/4 cup olive oil
2 tablespoons coarse sea salt
12 ounces celery root
Juice of 1/2 lemon
3 tablespoons walnut oil
8 ounces corn salad (or mixed salad leaves)
Salt & freshly ground black pepper

For the dressing
1 egg yolk
2 tablespoons Dijon mustard
1 tablespoon white wine vinegar
1 teaspoon soft brown sugar
5 tablespoons vegetable oil
1 tablespoon finely chopped fresh dill, plus a few sprigs to garnish
2 ounces dolcelatte cheese

Alternative cheeses
Dunsyre Blue, Danish Blue, Blue Castello (AUS), Dorset Blue or Yorkshire Blue

Cut the beef tenderloin into wafer-thin slices across the grain. If you find it difficult to slice the meat this thinly, cut thicker slices, place them between 2 sheets of oiled plastic wrap and beat out carefully with a rolling pin or meat pounder. Spread the slices in a single layer over 4 large serving plates. Sprinkle with the olive oil, coarse salt and some freshly ground black pepper.

For the dressing, put the egg yolk in a bowl and whisk in the mustard, vinegar and sugar. Gradually add the oil in a thin stream, whisking all the time, as if making mayonnaise. Stir in the chopped dill. Put the dolcelatte in a separate bowl, pour on 2 tablespoons of boiling water, and mix to a smooth paste. Add this paste to the dressing, blending it in well. Adjust the seasoning carefully, as the dolcelatte will be quite salty.

Peel the celery root, then shred it coarsely or cut it into fine strips (a mandolin is useful for this). Put it in a bowl, toss with the lemon juice and walnut oil, and season to taste.

To serve, toss the corn salad with the dressing and arrange on top of the beef, then sprinkle the celery root over. Garnish with sprigs of dill.

PG TIPS
Chill the beef briefly in the freezer to make it easier to slice. If the prospect of slicing and salting the beef seems daunting, try using a cured meat such as Bresaola or even prosciutto—they both work well. The crisp, nutty texture of the celery root lends a special flavor to the dish. Make every effort to get hold of some; you will not be disappointed!

chapter 2 **soups**

Some people are quite purist about what should go in a vichysoisse, which traditionally is made with leek and potato, but I think this version is definitely worthy of consideration. Intense yet delicate in flavor, it makes an ideal soup for early autumn. Like the original, it's thickened with cream and served chilled, garnished with chives.

pear, celery root & **stilton** vichysoisse

SERVES 4

2 tablespoons unsalted butter
1 onion, finely diced
3 cups peeled & finely diced celery root
2 ripe pears, peeled, cored & finely diced
1 quart Chicken Stock (see page 16) or Vegetable Stock (see page 16)
3 cups light cream
3/4 cup crumbled Stilton cheese
2 tablespoons chopped fresh chives
Salt & freshly ground black pepper

Alternative cheeses
Oregon Blue, Shropshire Blue, dolcelatte, Milawa Blue (AUS), Gippsland Tarago River Blue (AUS)

Heat the butter in a pan, add the onion and celery root and cook over a gentle heat until they begin to soften, about 8–10 minutes. Stir in the pears and cook for 3–4 minutes. Add the stock and bring to a boil, then reduce the heat and simmer for 25 minutes, until the vegetables are tender. Remove from the heat; stir in the cream and Stilton and then purée the soup in a blender until smooth. Let cool, then chill thoroughly.

Before serving it may be necessary to thin down the soup with a little milk, stock or cream. Stir in the chives and season to taste.

PG TIPS
I'm often asked what is the correct consistency for puréed soups. In my experience, a good general rule is that they should be approximately the consistency of light cream, that is thick enough to coat the back of a spoon.

These cloud-like cheese meringues not only taste great but also make a lovely presentation for this delicate, peppery-tasting pea soup.

pea & watercress soup with **emmenthal** floating islands

SERVES 4

4 tablespoons unsalted butter
1/2 cup roughly chopped onion
1 leek, roughly chopped
1 quart Chicken Stock
  (see page 16)
3 cups shelled fresh or
  frozen peas
2 bunches of watercress, tough
  stems removed
2 egg whites
3/4 cup freshly grated Emmenthal
  cheese, plus extra to serve
2 1/2 cups milk
2/3 cup double cream
Salt & freshly ground black pepper

Heat the butter in a heavy-based pan, add the onion and leek, and cook gently for 4–5 minutes, until softened. Add the stock and bring to a boil. Add the peas and simmer until tender–the cooking time will depend on whether you are using fresh or frozen peas. Stir in the watercress, then pour the soup into a blender and blitz until very smooth. For a more refined finish, strain it through a fine sieve afterwards.

Whisk the egg whites until they form stiff peaks and gently fold in the grated cheese. Use 2 tablespoons to shape the mixture into quenelles: To do this, take a heaped tablespoon of the mixture and then shape it with the second spoon, turning it between the two. Or you can just scoop it into 8–12 balls. Bring the milk to a simmer in a large pan. Poach the quenelles in it for 3–4 minutes, until set, turning them over halfway through. Remove with a slotted spoon and drain well.

Add the cream to the soup and reheat without letting it boil, then season to taste. Pour into warm bowls and serve topped with the cheese meringues and some shavings of Emmenthal.

PG TIPS
You could poach the floating islands in water, but they have a better flavor if you use milk. Save the milk afterwards to make a cheese sauce, if you like.

Sometimes known as French Cheddar, Cantal is a very versatile cooking cheese and is particularly good in soups, sauces, and gratins. It is at its best in late summer, when the milk is at its richest. Winter vegetables such as cabbage and carrots are often added to this soup along with the potatoes. I like to serve it with thin slices of toasted baguette rubbed with oil and garlic.

potato & **cantal** soup

SERVES 4

4 tablespoons unsalted butter
1½ pounds potatoes, cut into slices
  ½ inch thick
2½ cups leeks, white part only,
  thinly sliced
3 garlic cloves, crushed
2½ cups Chicken Stock or
  Vegetable Stock (see page 16)

⅓ cup heavy cream
1¼ cups milk, boiled & strained
1½ cups mature Cantal cheese
Salt & freshly Ground black pepper

Alternative cheeses
Beaufort, Gruyère, or Emmenthal

Heat the butter in a large saucepan, add the potatoes, leeks, and garlic. Cover and sweat for 4–5 minutes. Pour in the stock and bring to a boil. Skim to remove any impurities from the surface, then reduce the heat and simmer until the vegetables are just cooked. Add the cream and boiled milk and heat through gently, then stir in the grated Cantal. Remove from the heat, season to taste, and serve.

This rustic Italian soup is very nourishing and quick and easy to make. All you do is pour a well-flavored broth over slices of fried bread and then slip in an egg, which cooks in the heat of the broth. However, such simplicity relies on the finest ingredients for its success: Don't make the soup unless you have homemade stock, good country-style bread, and fresh free-range eggs.

zuppa pavese

SERVES 4

6 fresh eggs
8 slices of white country-style bread,
  cut ½ inch thick
1 cup freshly grated Parmesan
4 tablespoons unsalted butter
1 quart Meat Stock (see page 17) or,
  better still, consommé
Salt & freshly ground black pepper

Beat 2 of the eggs in a bowl, season lightly, and pour into a shallow dish. Dip the bread slices in the beaten egg on both sides, then dredge in ¾ cup of the grated Parmesan. Heat the butter in a large frying pan and fry the bread until golden on both sides.

Put the slices of fried bread in 4 deep, heatproof serving bowls. Bring the stock or consommé to a boil and pour it over the bread to immerse it completely. Crack an egg into each bowl on top of the bread. Leave the bowls on the side of the stove or over a very low heat to allow the eggs to cook lightly. Serve with the remaining cheese on the side, for sprinkling over the soup.

PG TIPS
If you prefer, you can poach the eggs in the hot stock in a saucepan, then place them on the fried bread in the soup bowls and pour the soup over.

This soup dates back to my early days at Inigo Jones restaurant in London's Covent Garden. I enjoy preparing and tasting it as much now as I did then. You can make the soup without the oysters and it's still good, but they do give it an incomparable scent and flavor.

white cabbage & oyster broth with
fourme d'ambert cheese

SERVES 4

4 tablespoons unsalted butter
2 heaped cups white cabbage, cut into 3/4-inch cubes
1 teaspoon cumin seeds
1 quart Vegetable Stock or Chicken Stock (see page 16)
12 fresh oysters
2 ounces Fourme d'Ambert
5 tablespoons heavy cream
1 tablespoon chopped fresh chives (optional)
Salt & freshly ground black pepper

Alternative cheeses
Dunsyre Blue, Cashel Blue, or Dovedale

Melt the butter in a saucepan, add the cabbage, then cover and sweat for 5–8 minutes. Stir in the cumin seeds, pour in the stock and bring to a boil. Skim off any impurities that rise to the surface, then simmer gently for about 15 minutes, until the cabbage is tender.

Meanwhile, open the oyster shells and remove the oysters, reserving their juice (see Tip on page 30). Cut the oysters in half, and strain the juice through a piece of cheesecloth. Set aside.

Press the Fourme d'Ambert cheese through a fine sieve and blend it with the cream. Stir the cream into the soup and adjust the seasoning. Add the cleaned oysters together with their strained juice, sprinkle with the chives, if using, and serve immediately.

PG TIPS
On no account let the soup boil after the cheese and cream mixture has been added to it or the delicate flavor will be spoiled. If the briny taste of oysters is not to your liking, you may prefer to substitute mussels. Simply cook the mussels with a little water until they open, then strain the cooking juices into the soup.

A warming, lightly spiced soup topped with stringy fontina cheese and spiked with lemon. Serve with chunks of fresh bread.

cannellini bean soup with **fontina gremolata**

SERVES 4

4 tablespoons unsalted butter
1/2 cup diced onions
1 garlic clove, minced
1 cup dried cannellini beans, soaked
   overnight & then drained
1/2 cup diced carrot
1/2 hot red chili pepper, seeded
   & minced
2 ripe tomatoes, chopped
2 cardamom pods, crushed
1 teaspoon cumin seeds
5 1/2 cups Chicken Stock or
   Vegetable Stock (see page 16)
Salt & freshly ground black pepper

For the gremolata
3/4 cup very finely grated
   fontina cheese
1 tablespoon finely grated
   lemon zest
1 tablespoon fresh thyme leaves
2 garlic cloves, crushed

Alternative cheeses
Raclette, Taleggio, Port Salut, or
Cornish Yarg

Melt the butter in a pan over a medium heat, add the onions and garlic and sauté for 4–5 minutes, until softened. Add the cannellini beans, carrot, chili, and tomatoes, then cover and cook gently for 5 minutes. Next, stir in the cardamom, cumin seeds, and stock and bring to a boil. Reduce the heat and simmer for 1–1 1/2 hours, or until the beans are tender. Pour the soup into a blender and blitz to a purée, then strain it through a fine sieve to give a creamy texture. Adjust the seasoning and reheat gently.

For the gremolata, mix all the ingredients together in a bowl. Pour the soup into warm bowls, scatter the gremolata over and serve right away.

PG TIPS
Other legumes such as lentils can be used with just as good effect. I sometimes leave the beans whole and top them with the gremolata to serve as a winter stew.

The surprising thing about this recipe is the stunning contrast of hot and cold. The chilled smooth gazpacho is poured around stuffed tomatoes that have come straight from the oven. The soup is strongly scented with basil, which I love to use in large quantities, but you can always reduce the amount if you prefer or if you don't have much available.

tomato gazpacho with **cabécou**-stuffed tomatoes

SERVES 4

2 pounds overripe plum tomatoes
 (or use half plum tomatoes, half
 beef tomatoes)
1 tablespoon tomato ketchup
1 tablespoon olive oil
1 small garlic clove, peeled
1 tablespoon sugar
2/3 cup Vegetable Stock (see page 16)
A bunch of fresh basil
2 tablespoons red wine vinegar
2 tablespoons dry vermouth
Salt & freshly ground white pepper

For the stuffed tomatoes
2 Cabécou cheeses or other small,
 firm goat cheeses
1/2 onion, minced
1 small zucchini, very finely chopped
1 egg yolk
1/2 cup mixed fresh herbs, such as
 basil, chervil, parsley, & chives,
 finely chopped
2–3 tablespoons fresh white
 bread crumbs
8 ripe but firm small tomatoes
A little olive oil for brushing

For the soup, blanch the tomatoes in boiling water for 1 minute, then drain and refresh in ice-cold water. Drain again and peel. Cut the tomatoes in half and put them in a bowl with the tomato ketchup, olive oil, garlic, sugar, vegetable stock, and leaves from the bunch of basil, reserving 8–12 leaves for garnishing the finished dish. Stir in the red wine vinegar and vermouth, season lightly and leave to marinate for 1–2 hours.

Strain the tomato mixture through a fine sieve into a bowl, pressing hard to extract all the juice (don't use a blender or the fresh color of the tomatoes will be lost). Adjust the seasoning, then chill until ready to serve.

For the stuffed tomatoes, preheat the oven to 350°F. Put the goat cheese in a bowl and crush with a fork. Stir in the onion, zucchini, egg yolk and herbs, then add enough breadcrumbs to bind the mixture lightly together. Season to taste. Slice a lid off the top of each tomato and reserve. Carefully scoop out the pulp and seeds from the tomatoes with a spoon. Fill them with the stuffing, brush with a little olive oil and bake for 5 minutes, until soft and heated through.

Place 2 stuffed tomatoes in each soup plate and replace their lids, then carefully pour the gazpacho around. Decorate with the reserved basil leaves and serve immediately.

PG TIPS
Make this soup in late summer when overripe tomatoes are being sold off cheaply. I strongly recommend that you keep this delicate, fresh-tasting soup for the summer months, as tomatoes have less flavor, juice and sweetness in winter.

According to a recent survey, by far the most popular vegetable dish in the UK is cauliflower cheese. So why not try cauliflower cheese soup?

cauliflower **cheese** soup

SERVES 4

1 large head cauliflower, weighing
  about 1 pound 10 ounces
4 tablespoons unsalted butter
1 onion, thinly sliced
1 leek, thinly sliced
1 quart Vegetable Stock (see
  page 16) or water
2 egg yolks
1/4 cup heavy cream
3/4 cup grated Wisconsin
  Cheddar cheese
Freshly grated nutmeg
Salt & freshly ground black pepper

Alternative cheeses
A soft goat cheese or Yorkshire Blue,
Buxton Blue or Gorwydd Caerphilly

Trim the outer green leaves off the cauliflower and cut it into florets. Heat the butter in a heavy-based saucepan, add the onion and leek, cover, and cook gently for 2–3 minutes, until the vegetables begin to soften. Do not let them brown. Add the cauliflower florets (reserving a few small ones as a garnish) and cook gently for 4–5 minutes. Pour in the stock or water and bring to a boil, then reduce the heat and simmer for 20–25 minutes, until the cauliflower is very tender. Meanwhile, cook the reserved cauliflower florets in boiling salted water until just tender. Drain, refresh in cold water, then drain again well and reserve.

Purée the soup in a blender until smooth. Return it to the saucepan and bring to a boil. In a bowl, lightly whisk together the egg yolks, cream, and cheese. Whisk about 6 tablespoons of the soup into this mixture, then stir it back into the remainder of the soup; do not let it boil. Season with nutmeg, salt and pepper, then serve garnished with the cooked cauliflower florets.

Here a rustic soup made from the humble potato is transformed into something magical with the addition of creamy sainte maure goat cheese, lifted with a little truffle oil.

potato & **sainte maure** soup with truffle oil

SERVES 4

4 tablespoons unsalted butter
1 onion, chopped
7 ounces leeks, sliced
7 ounces new potatoes, peeled
  & diced
4 cups chicken stock
1/2 cup heavy cream
3 ounces sainte maure goat cheese
  or any creamy goat cheese
1 tablespoon white truffle oil
Salt & freshly ground black pepper

Heat the butter in a large pan, add the onion and leeks, and cook over a low heat for 8–10 minutes without coloring. Add the potatoes and cook for another 3 minutes. Add the prepared stock and bring to a boil. Then reduce the heat and cook for 15 minutes or until tender.

In a separate pan heat the cream to a boil, then stir in the cheese and allow it to melt.

Place the potato soup in a blender and blitz to a purée. Mix in the goat cheese cream and the truffle oil. Season to taste and serve immediately.

PG TIPS

As an alternative to potato, Jerusalem artichoke and cauliflower are equally successful. The soup should be the consistency of light cream. If it is too thick, simply thin down with more chicken stock.

Lincolnshire Poacher is a full-flavored, unpasteurized milk cheese with a similar taste to a classic Cheddar, but with a more open texture. With its pale yellow hue and incredible brown rind, it has won numerous awards. Substitute with Tillamook Cheddar cheese.

lobster & **lincolnshire poacher** bisque

SERVES 4

1 cooked lobster, weighing
  about 1 1/2 pounds
6 tablespoons unsalted butter
1/2 onion, roughly chopped
1 celery stalk, roughly chopped
1 carrot, roughly chopped
2 garlic cloves, minced
2 tablespoons tomato paste
1/4 cup cognac
2/3 cup dry white wine
1 tablespoon fresh tarragon leaves,
  plus a few sprigs to garnish
75g plain flour
1 litre Chicken Stock (see page 16)
2/3 cup heavy cream
3/4 cup grated Lincolnshire Poacher
  or Tillamook Cheddar
Cayenne pepper
Salt & freshly ground black pepper

Split the lobster in half down the back: the easiest way to do this is to put a large knife through the center of the body section and cut down through the head, then take out the knife, turn the lobster around, and cut down the center of the body through the tail. Remove and discard the head sac and the intestinal vein, then remove the cooked lobster meat from the head and tail. Crack the claws in 2 or 3 places and pick out the meat. Place the lobster shells in a bowl and, using a meat pounder, crush them into smallish pieces. This helps to extract maximum flavor.

Heat the butter in a heavy-based pan, add the crushed lobster shells, and fry for 4–5 minutes, until they begin to turn golden. Add the vegetables and garlic and fry for 5 minutes, until softened. Stir in the tomato paste, then add the cognac, white wine and tarragon leaves and cook for 5 minutes. Stir in the flour and cook for a further 5 minutes. Add the stock, bring to a boil and skim off any impurities that rise to the surface. Reduce the heat and simmer for 30–40 minutes.

Meanwhile, dice the lobster meat and set aside. Bring the cream to a boil in a separate pan, then remove from the heat. Add the cheese and stir until melted and smooth, then set aside.

Blitz the soup in a blender until the shells are quite finely ground, then pass it through a very fine sieve and stir in the cheese cream. Add cayenne, salt and pepper to taste, then pour the soup into warm bowls. Garnish with the diced lobster meat and sprigs of tarragon, dust very lightly with cayenne and serve.

PG TIPS
Rice may be used instead of flour to thicken the soup. It is important that you do not cook the stock for longer than 40 minutes, as it will lose its natural flavors and become bitter. If you decide to use crab instead of lobster, cook the live crabs for 12–15 minutes, depending on their size.

Like Zuppa Pavese (see page 54), this is an Italian peasant-style soup. I love the simplicity of it, made with just a few basic ingredients and a little care. It makes thrifty use of leftovers but it is essential to have good-quality stock and good-quality olive oil. And you should not neglect the lemon; however strange it may sound, it really does give a little lift to this substantial, warming soup.

bread & **pecorino** soup

SERVES 4

1 quart Chicken Stock (see page 16)
4 tablespoons olive oil
2 garlic cloves, minced
2 cups potatoes, peeled & cut into small cubes
4 thick slices of stale Italian country bread, cut into cubes

6 tablespoons grated pecorino
1 tablespoon coarsely chopped fresh marjoram
1/4 teaspoon grated lemon zest
Salt
Cracked black pepper (see Tip on page 146)

Bring the stock to a boil with 3 tablespoons of the olive oil, add the garlic and potatoes and return to a boil. Add the bread cubes and simmer for 20–25 minutes, until the potatoes are tender. Remove the pan from the heat and stir in the pecorino, marjoram and lemon zest. Season with a little salt and a sprinkling of freshly cracked black pepper. Drizzle the remaining olive oil over and serve right away.

This variation on the classic French onion soup replaces the usual white wine and Gruyère with ingredients from Normandy–beer and Camembert cheese. I have successfully replaced the Camembert with Carré de l'Est, which is milder in flavor and has a delicate aroma when ripe. You can, of course, use grated Gruyère or Emmenthal for a more traditional onion soup.

french onion soup with beer & **camembert**

SERVES 4

6 tablespoons unsalted butter
3 cups finely sliced onion
1/2 tablespoon sugar
1 tablespoon all-purpose flour
1 teaspoon tomato paste
1/2 cup light beer
1 quart Meat Stock (see page 17)

1 ficelle (small, thin baguette) or 2 crusty bread rolls, thinly sliced & toasted
4 ounces Camembert cheese, rind removed, thinly sliced
Salt & freshly ground black pepper

Alternative cheeses
Carré de l'Est, Gruyère, Emmenthal

Heat the butter in a heavy-based pan, add the onions and sugar, and cook over a medium heat for at least 20 minutes, until very soft, golden, and caramelized. Stir in the flour and tomato paste and cook for 2 minutes, until they brown very slightly. Pour in the beer and bring to a boil and after 1 minute add the stock. Reduce the heat and simmer for 15–20 minutes, then season to taste. Pour the soup into 4 heatproof soup bowls or 1 large tureen and float the toasted bread on top in a single layer. Cover this with the Camembert slices. Put the bowls under the broiler (or in a hot oven) until the cheese forms a well-browned crust. Serve immediately.

A beautifully delicate vegetable chowder spiked with aromatic saffron and cilantro. Saffron is now much more readily available, and imports from Spain and the Middle East continue to improve. It is an expensive spice but it has no substitute, especially in this chowder. Sachets of powdered saffron are cheaper than saffron strands but they cannot compete with them in flavor—always buy the real thing.

saffron vegetable chowder with cilantro & **goat cheese** pesto

SERVES 4

3 tablespoons olive oil
1 garlic clove, minced
1 leek, 1 carrot, 1 celery stalk,
  1 zucchini, 1 potato, all cut into
  $1/4$ inch dice
1 quart Vegetable Stock
  or Chicken Stock (see page 16)
A pinch of saffron strands
2 tomatoes, skinned, seeded, & cut
  into $1/4$ inch cubes
2 tablespoons Cilantro & Goat
  Cheese Pesto (see page 20)
$1/2$ cup milk
Salt & freshly ground black pepper

Heat the olive oil in a heavy-based pan, together with the garlic. Next, add the leek, carrot, celery, zucchini, and potato and cook for 2 minutes over a low heat.

Add the stock and saffron and bring to a boil. Reduce the heat and simmer for 20–25 minutes, until the vegetables are tender. Add the tomatoes and pesto and stir thoroughly, then add the milk. Season to taste with salt and pepper and serve immediately.

PG TIPS
As an effective variation, replace the cilantro and goat cheese pesto with fresh herbs, such as parsley, basil, or chives.

chapter 3 **salads**

The simplest of tomato salads, topped with a creamy dressing made with goat cheese and goat's milk. Serve as an accompaniment or as part of a selection of salads for a picnic.

plum tomato salad with **goat's milk** dressing

SERVES 4

8 large, ripe, but firm plum
  tomatoes, cut into slices
  1/4 inch thick
3 ounces Roubiliac or Golden Cross
  goat cheese
1/3 cup goat's milk
2 tablespoons Greek yogurt
1 tablespoon chopped fresh basil
1 tablespoon chopped fresh oregano
1/2 tablespoon chopped fresh
  cilantro
Salt & freshly ground black pepper

Arrange the tomato slices in overlapping circles in a shallow serving bowl. Season with salt and pepper. Whisk all the remaining ingredients together and pour over the tomatoes. Serve well chilled.

PG TIPS

If you can't find goat's milk, cow's milk works well, too. I personally see no gain in removing the tomato skins for this salad, especially in summer when tomatoes are at their best. It is, of course, a matter of choice, and others may like to blanch them briefly in boiling water before peeling off the skins. Chives, parsley, or chervil would make excellent alternative herbs, but they must be fresh.

I love the smoky flavors that predominate in this salad. The tart vinaigrette makes an ideal dressing for the charred leeks. If possible, grill the vegetables over charcoal.

blackened leek, red onion & smoked **mozzarella** salad with tarragon vinaigrette

SERVES 4

A pinch of sugar
24 young leeks, trimmed
2 red onions, cut into wedges
1 smoked mozzarella cheese, cut
  into 8 thin slices
Salt & freshly ground black pepper

For the vinaigrette
3 tablespoons tarragon vinegar
  or champagne vinegar
1 teaspoon Dijon mustard
1 tablespoon chopped fresh tarragon
9 tablespoons extra-virgin olive oil
1 tomato, seeded & finely diced
1 tablespoon superfine capers,
  rinsed & drained
1 tablespoon green olives, pitted &
  minced
1 hard-boiled egg, chopped

Alternative cheeses
Buffalo mozzarella or a goat
  cheese, such as coarsely
  grated crottin

Bring a large pan of water to a boil with the sugar and a little salt. Throw in the leeks, return to a boil and cook gently for 2–3 minutes. Drain them well and dry on a cloth.

For the vinaigrette, mix the vinegar, mustard, and tarragon together in a bowl and then whisk in the olive oil. Add all the remaining ingredients and season to taste with salt and pepper.

Grill the leeks and onions—for the best flavor this should be done over charcoal or a ridged cast-iron grill pan, but you can also cook them under the broiler. When they are tender and slightly blackened, remove from the heat and season with salt and pepper.

Toss the leeks and onions with the vinaigrette and adjust the seasoning. Arrange on 4 serving plates, drape 2 slices of mozzarella over each portion and serve.

PG TIPS
Smoked mozzarella may not be a recognised household cheese, yet for me it is one of the nicest smoked cheeses. It is worth seeking out but, if you have a problem finding it, a creamy-tasting natural mozzarella would be fine.

The dark greeny-blue French lentilles du Puy are generally considered to have the best flavor and are well worth buying. They have recently been granted appellation d'origine contrôlée status, just like a fine wine or cheese, which means that only lentils from a particular corner of France—the area around Puy-en-Velay in the Haute Loire—are entitled to be called Puy. This decree is causing consternation among some British supermarket chains, which sell "Puy lentils" that have in fact been produced in Canada. If you can't get the genuine article, don't worry! Cannellini beans also work very well in this winter salad.

warm lentil salad with pepper-grilled **goat cheese** & anchovy toasts

SERVES 4

1 cup Puy lentils
1 onion, minced
1 teaspoon cumin seeds
¼ cup olive oil
2 tablespoons balsamic vinegar or
  white wine vinegar
1 shallot, minced

For the toasts
6 canned anchovy fillets, rinsed
  & dried
1 egg yolk
5 tablespoons olive oil
4 slices of French bread,
  cut ⅔ inch thick
4 Montrachet goat cheeses, cut
  horizontally in half
1 tablespoon fresh thyme or
  rosemary leaves
1 tablespoon coarsely ground
  black peppercorns

Alternative cheese
4 crottins, cut horizontally in half
or Tasmania Highland Chevre
(AUS)

Put the lentils in a saucepan, cover with cold water, and bring to a boil, skimming off any impurities that rise to the surface. Add the onion and cumin seeds and simmer for 30–40 minutes, until the lentils are just tender. Drain them well. Mix the olive oil, vinegar, and shallot together and stir into the lentils. Keep warm.

For the cheese and anchovy toasts, work the anchovies and egg yolk to a paste with a mortar and pestle, then gradually blend in the olive oil to make a thick purée. Toast the French bread and spread with the anchovy paste, then top each one with 2 pieces of goat cheese. Sprinkle with the thyme or rosemary leaves and black pepper and place under the broiler until lightly browned. Put the warm lentils on serving plates, top with the toasts, and serve right away.

PG TIPS
Because the quantities for the anchovy paste are small, you really need to use a mortar and pestle. However, if you double the amount, you can blitz everything together in a blender. You are bound to find a use for the surplus; store it in the refrigerator and toss with pasta or use in sandwiches.

For me, the combination of spinach and blue cheese is a spectacular one. Any type of blue cheese is suitable for this wonderfully fresh-tasting salad, scattered with nutritious pumpkin seeds. Just use your favorite.

spinach, **blue cheese** & avocado salad with pumpkin seeds

SERVES 4

12 ounces tender young spinach
  leaves (about 3¹/₂ cups
1¹/₂ cups sliced mushrooms
2 hard-boiled eggs, chopped
⁴/₅ cup blue cheese, in ¹/₂ inch cubes
1 garlic clove, minced
Scant 1 cup fromage blanc
1 teaspoon mild Dijon mustard
1 teaspoon lemon juice
1 avocado, peeled, pitted & cut into
  ¹/₂ inch cubes
12 slices of small baguette, toasted
¹/₂ cup pumpkin seeds, toasted
Salt & freshly ground black pepper

Put the spinach in a salad bowl and add the mushrooms, hard-boiled eggs, and blue cheese. Mix together the garlic, fromage blanc, mustard, and lemon juice to make a dressing and toss carefully with the salad. Season to taste.

Arrange on serving plates, top with the avocado and toasted baguette slices and sprinkle the toasted pumpkin seeds over. Serve immediately.

PG TIPS
Other vegetables, such as leeks, artichokes, and even asparagus, can be prepared in the same way for this salad. Pumpkin seeds are quite easy to find in health food shops, but sunflower seeds make a tasty alternative if necessary.

Jarlsberg cheese is said by many to be a copy of the famous Swiss Emmenthal. I personally think it has a more delicate flavor and not such a nutty aftertaste. It is one of Norway's proudest treasures and deserves to be better known and more frequently used.

salad of pickled herrings, **jarlsberg**, potatoes & dill

SERVES 4

1 pound pickled herrings
1 pound waxy potatoes
1 red onion, minced
2 tablespoons white wine vinegar
6 tablespoons olive oil
1 tablespoon crème fraîche

2 tablespoons chopped fresh dill
1 tablespoon sweet German mustard
5 ounces Jarlsberg
Salt & freshly ground black pepper

Alternative cheeses
Emmenthal, Cheddar, Havarti,
or Tilsit

Cut the pickled herrings into large chunks and the Jarlsberg into sticks. Cook the potatoes in boiling salted water until just tender, then drain. Leave until cool enough to handle, then peel and cut in half. Put them in a bowl and add the herrings and red onion. Mix together the vinegar, oil, crème fraîche, dill, and mustard to make a dressing. Pour the dressing over the potatoes, herrings, and onions and toss lightly together, then season to taste. Transfer to a serving bowl, top with the sticks of Jarlsberg and serve.

I am very fond of this salad. It always finds a place on my winter menus and is extremely pretty. The crunch of red cabbage and roasted walnuts makes an excellent combination with the sharp and tangy Roquefort. If Roquefort is not available, any blue cheese could be substituted, but I find the stronger ones such as Gorgonzola work best.

roquefort & red cabbage salad with roasted walnut vinaigrette

SERVES 4

1/4 red cabbage, central core
   removed, thinly sliced
1/4 cup red wine vinegar
1/4 cup sugar
2 1/2 cups water
4 ounces (4 slices) streaky bacon,
   cut into 3/4 inch dice
2 slices of white bread, cut into
   1/2 inch cubes
1 garlic clove, minced
2 heads Belgian endive
1 small head of radicchio
1 heaped cup crumbled
   Roquefort cheese
Salt & freshly ground black pepper

For the vinaigrette
1/4 cup red wine vinegar
1 teaspoon Dijon mustard
1/4 cup walnut oil
1/4 cup olive oil
2 tablespoons roasted walnuts (see
   Tip), broken into chunks

Alternative cheeses
Any blue cheese, especially Valdeon

Put the cabbage in a bowl. Bring the vinegar to a boil, add the sugar, and, once dissolved, pour it over the cabbage and stir well. Boil the water and pour that over the cabbage too. Leave to soak for 5 minutes, then drain in a colander and let cool.

Heat a frying pan over a high heat, add the bacon, and cook until it is crisp and the fat has been released. Add the bread and fry until golden, then stir in the garlic and fry for 1 minute. Remove from the heat. Put the red cabbage in a salad bowl with the endive and radicchio leaves, scatter over the bacon and croûtons, and the Roquefort cheese.

Whisk together all the ingredients for the vinaigrette and pour it over the salad. Toss well, adjust the seasoning and serve.

PG TIPS
To roast nuts, toss them in a little oil, season lightly, then place on a baking sheet and bake in an oven preheated to 350°F for 5–8 minutes, or until toasted in flavor and color. Cool before use. I have on occasion replaced the red cabbage with finely shredded beets: a great alternative summer salad.

Many years ago I worked in the west country of England and discovered just how good the fresh crab can be there. It has an incomparable flavor. The salad makes a good first course for an early-summer meal.

crab & asparagus salad with lemon, mustard & **parmesan** vinaigrette

SERVES 4

12 asparagus spears, peeled &
  well trimmed
2 heads Belgian endive
2 avocados, peeled, pitted & sliced
2 carrots, cut into matchsticks
11 ounces fresh white crabmeat
  (about 2 cups)
Parmesan shavings, to garnish
Salt & freshly ground black pepper

For the lemon, mustard &
Parmesan vinaigrette
1 tablespoon Dijon mustard
1 medium egg yolk
1 tablespoon lemon juice
Finely grated zest of 1/4 lemon
1 tablespoon champagne vinegar or
  white wine vinegar
5 tablespoons extra-virgin olive oil
1 1/2 tablespoons freshly grated
  Parmesan

Cook the asparagus spears in boiling salted water for 3–4 minutes or until just tender. Drain and refresh in cold water, then dry them thoroughly and cut lengthwise in half.

For the dressing, whisk together the mustard, egg yolk, lemon juice and zest and vinegar, then whisk in the olive oil. Add the grated Parmesan cheese and season to taste.

Pull the leaves from the endive, wash and dry them and arrange in a salad bowl or on serving plates. Put the asparagus, avocado, carrots, and crabmeat in a separate bowl and toss gently with the dressing, then adjust the seasoning. Scatter this mixture over the endive leaves, sprinkle with some coarsely cracked black pepper (see Tip on page 146), then scatter with the Parmesan shavings. Serve immediately.

PG TIPS
Vegetarians can easily omit the crabmeat and replace it with more vegetables. Globe artichoke hearts, for example, would go rather well.

In this tangy salad the oranges are marinated in vinegar and sugar overnight to give a refreshing sweet-and-sour flavor. Feta is a much-copied cheese and consequently the quality and flavor vary greatly, as does the type of milk used. Always try to obtain genuine Greek feta, which is generally made of 30 per cent goat's milk and 70 per cent sheep's milk.

chili-pickled orange, **feta** & olive salad

SERVES 4

4 oranges, preferably navel
1/3 cup white wine vinegar
3 tablespoons sugar
1 hot red chili peppper, thinly sliced
  into rings
1/3 cup olive oil
2 tablespoons black olives, pitted
3/4 cup feta, cut into 1/2 inch cubes
1 tablespoon chopped fresh oregano
  or parsley
Baby spinach and arugula leaves, to
  garnish (optional)
Salt & freshly ground black pepper

Alternative cheeses
Haloumi or a firm goat cheese

Peel the oranges, being sure to remove all the white pith, and cut them into slices 1/4 inch thick. Remove any seeds and put the orange slices in a shallow dish. Boil the vinegar and sugar together for 2–3 minutes, then add the chili pepper and then pour over the orange slices. Cover and leave overnight.

The next day, drain off the juices from the pickled oranges into a bowl. Whisk in the olive oil to make a dressing and season with salt and pepper. Arrange the oranges in a serving bowl. Stir the olives, feta, and oregano or parsley into the dressing and sprinkle it over the oranges. Sprinkle with coarsely cracked black pepper (see Tip on page 146), scatter over the spinach and arugula leaves, if using, and serve.

PG TIPS
Some people like to soak feta cheese in warm water or milk before using. This effectively softens the strong, salty flavor.

Radicchio is a bitter salad leaf that to my mind needs a contrasting partner. The blue cheese yogurt dressing fits the bill perfectly. You could add some chopped hard-boiled egg, potatoes and haricots verts beans to make a more substantial dish for a main course.

radicchio, mushroom & chive salad with **blue cheese** yogurt dressing

SERVES 4

2 heads of radicchio
5 cups button mushrooms, sliced
1 bunch of fresh chives
Salt & freshly ground black pepper

For the blue cheese yogurt dressing
2 ounces Stilton
1 tablespoon champagne vinegar
5 tablespoons crème fraîche
3 tablespoons strained plain yogurt
Juice of 1/2 lemon
Freshly grated nutmeg
1 tablespoon chopped fresh chives

Alternative cheeses
Roquefort, dolcelatte, or Cambazola

First make the dressing. Put the Stilton in a bowl and mash well with a fork. Stir in the vinegar, then gently whisk in the crème fraîche and yogurt. Squeeze in the lemon juice and season to taste with nutmeg, salt and pepper. Fold in the chives.

Separate the radicchio leaves, wash them, and dry them well. Place in a bowl, add the sliced mushrooms, and season lightly. Add the blue cheese dressing and toss carefully, then adjust the seasoning to taste. Arrange on serving plates, snip the chives into pieces 1/2 inch long and scatter over the top. Serve immediately.

PG TIPS
If you prefer a less tart dressing, add 1 tablespoon warmed honey, maple syrup or even good old sugar. Try adding a little grated orange zest to the dressing, too. Belgian endive or chicory has a similar bitter taste and could easily be substituted for the radicchio.

This hearty salad of cheese, ham, and potatoes is substantial enough to serve as a main course. Salads that combine cheese and meat are very common in northern Europe. I devised this one with Italian flavorings in mind. The recipe has been in my repertoire since my early days as a chef and has remained one of my favorite salads. The original salad consists of shavings of Tête de Moine (monk's head), a cheese native to Switzerland. It is rather expensive and a little difficult to find except in specialist cheese shops, but well worth enquiring about. Fontina makes a more accessible and good substitute.

insalata di **fontina**

SERVES 4

8 ounces new potatoes
2 ounces prosciutto, cut into strips
4 ounces fontina cheese, cut
  into sticks
2 ounces mortadella, cut into sticks
6 cocktail gherkins, cut lengthwise
  into quarters
1 red onion, sliced into thin rings
Salt & freshly ground black pepper

For the dressing
1 tablespoon chopped fresh oregano
1/4 teaspoon Dijon mustard
2 canned anchovy fillets
2 tablespoons white wine vinegar
6 tablespoons olive oil

Alternative cheeses
Gruyère, Emmenthal, Port Salut,
Jarlsberg, or Leerdammer

For the dressing, place the oregano and mustard in a small bowl. Rinse the anchovy fillets to reduce their salty flavor, then drain. Dry them well and mince. Add them to the bowl, pour over the vinegar and mix well together. Add the olive oil and whisk to form a light dressing. Season to taste and set aside.

Cook the potatoes in boiling salted water for about 20 minutes until just tender, then drain and cool slightly before peeling. Cut into 1/4 inch thick slices and place in a bowl. While the potatoes are still warm, pour the dressing over and leave for 20 minutes to let them soak up the flavors.

Add the remaining ingredients and mix together. Pour on the dressing and toss again. Adjust the seasoning and serve.

Lamb and mint form a combination that everyone knows. I took it a stage further to create this wonderful salad. We are fortunate that we can still buy the Scottish cheese Lanark Blue. In 1995 its producer, Humphrey Errington, fought a 13-month battle in the courts to defend its reputation against health officials, who claimed that as a raw-milk cheese it could contain the bacterium Listeria and thus cause food poisoning. He finally won his case, and small cheesemakers throughout the UK owe him a huge debt for demonstrating that cheese made from unpasteurized milk carries no more risk to health than pasteurized cheese.

salad of grilled lamb fillet with **lanark blue** & warm mint dressing

SERVES 4

4 boneless neck of lamb fillets,
  about 3 ounces each
4 ounces haricots verts
8–12 thin slices cut from a ficelle
  loaf or small baguette
Olive oil, for brushing
A handful each of curly endive
  & spinach leaves
2 tomatoes, skinned, seeded &
  cut into strips
1 cup thinly sliced button mushrooms
1/2 cup diced Lanark Blue cheese
Salt & freshly ground black pepper

For the dressing
1/4 cup heavy cream
1 tablespoon clear honey
1/2 cup crumbled Lanark Blue cheese
1 tablespoon sherry vinegar
2 tablespoons olive oil
1 tablespoon chopped fresh mint
2 tablespoons hot water

Alternative cheeses
Stilton, Danish Blue, Bleu
d'Auvergne, Buxton Blue, or King
Island (AUS)

Season the lamb fillets and grill on a ridged cast-iron grill pan (or cook under the broiler or in a frying pan) for 5–8 minutes, until done but still rosy inside. Keep warm.

Meanwhile, cook the beans in boiling salted water until just tender, then drain and refresh in cold water. Drain again and dry.

For the dressing, put the cream and honey in a pan and bring to a boil, then remove from the heat. Add the cheese and allow it to melt into the cream. Whisk in the vinegar, olive oil and mint, then whisk in the water and season to taste.

Brush the slices of bread with olive oil and toast on both sides on the grill pan or under the broiler until they are lightly browned.

Put the curly endive and spinach leaves in a bowl, add the tomatoes, French beans, mushrooms and cheese, then toss with the warm dressing. Put in the center of 4 serving plates. Slice the grilled lamb fillets and arrange around the salad. Top the salad with the croûtons and serve immediately.

chapter 4 **pasta, pizza, rice & gnocchi**

A great and simple dish. When all that is needed is something quick but tasty, this fits the bill perfectly. Try adding crisply fried, diced pancetta to the pasta.

tagliatelle with fried egg, capers & **pecorino** sardo

SERVES 4

1 pound tagliatelle
Freshly grated nutmeg
3 tablespoons unsalted butter
2 tablespoons superfine capers,
  rinsed & drained
4 free-range eggs
A little clarified butter (see Tip)
4 ounces pecorino Sardo cheese,
  cut into shavings
Salt & freshly ground black pepper

Cook the pasta in boiling salted water until al dente, then drain well and return to the pan. Season with nutmeg, salt and pepper, add the butter and capers, and toss together well. Keep warm.

Quickly fry the eggs in clarified butter and season with salt. Arrange the pasta on warmed serving plates, top each portion with a fried egg, and scatter over the pecorino shavings. Sprinkle with a little freshly cracked black pepper (see Tip on page 146) and serve.

PG TIPS
To clarify butter, heat gently in a small pan until it begins to boil. Boil for 2 minutes, then pour off the clear butter through a fine conical strainer or a cheesecloth-lined sieve, leaving the white, milky sediment in the pan. Store clarified butter in the refrigerator.

Make this dish during the autumnal months of the year, when a vast array of exciting mushrooms become available. If you are lucky enough to use wild mushrooms use 11 ounces of your favorite variety but, as these are not always within everyone's grasp, I have used the more commonly available dried mushrooms in the recipe.

funghi **carbonara**

SERVES 4

1 pound fresh/dried spaghetti
  or linguini
4 ounces diced pancetta
2 tablespoons unsalted butter
$3/4$ ounce dried mixed wild
  mushrooms (soaked in hot water
  for 1 hour)
1 shallot, finely chopped
$2/3$ cup heavy cream
2 eggs beaten
1 cup freshly grated parmesan
Salt, freshly ground pepper &
  ground nutmeg

Alternative cheese
Pecorino

Cook the pasta in a large pan of boiling salted water, until al dente, then drain well in a colander.

Fry the pancetta until crispy. Heat the butter in a large frying pan, drain the mushrooms from their water and add to the pan. Add the shallots and cook together for 3–4 minutes until softened. Add the pancetta.

Pour over the cream and cook for 2–3 minutes until the sauce has thickened slightly.

Add the drained pasta and stir in the beaten eggs and cheese. Toss well together and season with salt, pepper and nutmeg. Serve immediately.

Although I have used bucatini pasta for this recipe, other pastas such as linguini and fettucine are equally suitable. Whenever I make this simple dish at home it transports me to the Greek Islands in an instant. Hot pickled chili peppers are available from Middle Eastern specialty shops.

bucatini with **feta**, pickled chili, tomato & mint

SERVES 4

4 tablespoons good quality olive oil
1 small garlic clove, crushed
1 pound bucatini
3 tablespoons chopped fresh mint
4 ripe but firm plum tomatoes
  cut into 1/4-inch dice
2 cups Greek feta, cut into small
  1/4-inch dice
2 small hot pickled chili peppers,
  finely chopped

Alternative cheeses
Mozzarella

Heat half the oil in a large frying pan over a medium heat, add the garlic and cook for 1 minute until it becomes translucent. Stir in the mint, add the chopped tomatoes, and diced feta and cook for a further 2–3 minutes.

Meanwhile, cook the bucatini in a large pan of boiling salted water until al dente. Drain the pasta in a colander and add to the pan. Add the pickled chili peppers and toss the mixture together.

Divide the pasta between 4 serving pasta bowls and drizzle over the remaining oil.

PG TIPS
The addition of a few chopped black olives to this dish is very pleasing.

Crumbly cottage or curd cheese is used extensively in many German dishes. I particularly like the stuffing for this ravioli.

topfenravioli with prosciutto, spinach & foaming brown butter

SERVES 4

6 tablespoons unsalted butter
1 pound young spinach leaves
  (about 4 1/2 cups)
1/2 cup cottage cheese, well drained
3 ounces prosciutto, finely diced
  (about 3/4 cup)
1/4 cup buffalo or cow's milk
  mozzarella, finely diced
2 tablespoons freshly grated
  Parmesan, plus extra to serve
10 fresh basil leaves, roughly
  chopped, plus a few whole leaves
  to garnish
Freshly grated nutmeg
Salt & freshly ground black pepper

For the pasta dough
2 cups all-purpose flour
A pinch of salt
1 tablespoon extra-virgin olive oil
2 eggs plus 1 egg yolk, lightly beaten

First make the pasta dough. Put the flour, salt, and olive oil into a food processor and process for a few seconds to combine. Add the beaten eggs and process until the mixture forms a mass. This should only take a few seconds; it is important not to overwork the dough. Remove the dough from the food processor. It should be fairly soft and pliable. If it is too dry, knead in a little water; if it is too wet, sprinkle with a little flour. Cover with plastic wrap and let rest at room temperature for 15–30 minutes.

Meanwhile, make the filling. Heat 2 tablespoons of the butter in a large pan, add the spinach and cook for just a few minutes until it has wilted and all the excess moisture has evaporated. Transfer to a bowl and let cool, then mince. Stir in the cottage cheese, prosciutto, mozzarella, Parmesan, and chopped basil. Season to taste with nutmeg, salt and pepper.

Roll out the dough using a pasta machine if you have one. Alternatively, divide it into 2 batches and roll it out very thinly by hand. It should be so thin that it is almost translucent. Lightly brush 1 sheet of the dough with water, then put teaspoonfuls of stuffing on it about 2 inches apart, in rows. Cover with the second sheet of pasta and press down gently, then cut around the stuffing with a 2 1/2 inch fluted round pastry cutter. Check that the edges of the ravioli are well sealed.

Cook the ravioli in plenty of gently simmering salted water for 2–3 minutes, until al dente, then drain well. Heat the remaining butter in a frying pan until it is foaming and golden brown and smells nutty (the bottom of the pan will be covered with brown butter specks). Immediately drizzle the butter over the ravioli and sprinkle with more freshly grated Parmesan and a few basil leaves before serving.

For an all-green version of this colorful pasta dish, you could substitute zucchini, leeks, and broccoli for the sweet peppers.

rigatoni with mixed peppers & cilantro & **goat cheese** pesto

SERVES 4

4 sweet peppers (1 red, 1 green, 1 yellow, 1 orange)
4 tablespoons unsalted butter
2 tablespoons olive oil
A pinch of sugar
1 pound rigatoni
1 quantity of Cilantro & Goat Cheese Pesto (see page 20)
Salt & freshly ground black pepper
Fresh cilantro leaves, to garnish (optional)

Halve and seed the peppers, then cut them into strips ¼ inch wide. Heat the butter and oil in a frying pan, add the pepper strips and cook gently for 10–15 minutes. If they begin to stick to the pan, add a little water. When the peppers are tender, stir in the sugar, and salt and pepper to taste.

Cook the rigatoni in a large pan of boiling salted water until al dente, then drain well. Stir the pasta into the peppers, add the pesto sauce and lightly toss together. Adjust the seasoning, garnish with cilantro if liked, and serve immediately.

PG TIPS

For a really quick sauce, use bottled peppers (pimientos) in oil. For a little variation why not try adding a few sautéed bacon lardons to the cooked pasta? Any other shaped pasta would look pretty in this dish.

Although I have used pennette for this dish, any type of pasta can be substituted. To offset the richness of the sauce, I sometimes top the pasta with a light herb salad of basil, chives, and oregano, mixed with a little curly endive and dressed with balsamic vinaigrette.

pennette al **dolcelatte**

SERVES 4

1 pound pennette
⅓ cup heavy cream
½ cup Chicken Stock or Vegetable Stock (see page 16)
⅔ cup crumbled dolcelatte
¼ cup extra-virgin olive oil
Freshly grated nutmeg
Salt & freshly ground black pepper
Freshly grated Parmesan, to serve (optional)

Alternative cheese
Try dolcelatte torta, which is a combination of mascarpone and dolcelatte, and omit the double cream

Cook the pennette in plenty of boiling salted water until al dente. Meanwhile, bring the cream and stock to a boil, then remove from the heat and stir in the dolcelatte until smooth. Whisk in the olive oil to form a light sauce.

Drain the pasta and return it to the saucepan. Season with nutmeg, salt and pepper, then toss the pasta with the sauce. Serve immediately, with grated Parmesan if desired.

Calzone means pair of trousers! It is a folded pizza, rather like a turnover, and is particularly delicious if you include lots of cheese so the molten cheese spills out when you cut into it. You can vary the fillings to your own taste—try mozzarella, salami, or vegetables.

bel paese calzoni

SERVES 4

1 quantity of risen pizza dough
  (see opposite)
Flour, for dusting
2 tablespons ricotta cheese
2 garlic cloves, minced
2 tablespoons olive oil
3 ounces Bel Paese, rind removed,
  coarsely chopped
4 ounces mortadella or prosciutto,
  coarsely chopped (about 1 cup)
A little beaten egg
Vegetable oil for deep-frying
Salt & freshly ground black pepper

Punch down the risen dough, then roll it out thinly on a floured surface. Cut out eight 6-inch disks.

Mix together the ricotta, garlic, olive oil, Bel Paese, and chopped mortadella or prosciutto. Season to taste. Put the mixture on one half of each disk of dough, leaving a border. Brush the edges of the dough with beaten egg and fold over to make turnovers. Crimp the edges for a neat finish.

Heat the vegetable oil in a large saucepan and fry the calzoni a few at a time for 5–6 minutes, until golden. Alternatively, brush them with a little beaten egg and bake in an oven preheated to 400°F for about 12–15 minutes. Serve hot.

To me, these calzoni are lifted out of the ordinary by the inclusion of fennel, a much underrated vegetable which only the Italians seem to use to any extent. Serve the calzoni with a tomato sauce, if you like.

the ultimate vegetarian calzoni

SERVES 4

1 quantity of risen pizza dough
  (see opposite)
Flour, for dusting
6 tablespoons olive oil
1 garlic clove, crushed
1/4 teaspoon fennel seeds
1 eggplant, peeled & thinly sliced
1 fennel bulb, thinly sliced
5 ounces mozzarella, thinly sliced
10 basil leaves, roughly chopped
A little beaten egg
Vegetable oil for deep-frying
Salt & freshly ground black pepper

Punch down the risen dough, then roll it out thinly on a floured surface. Cut out eight 6-inch disks.

For the filling, heat the olive oil in a pan with the garlic and fennel seeds. Add the eggplant and fennel slices and cook gently for 12–15 minutes, until golden and tender. Add a little water to the vegetables if they begin to stick to the pan. Transfer to a bowl and let cool, then add the mozzarella and basil. Season to taste. Fill the turnovers, seal with a little beaten egg, and cook as in the preceding recipe.

A truly wonderful vegetarian pizza: roasted vegetables topped with contrasting cheeses and drizzled with rosemary oil. A real treat.

roasted vegetable pizza with goat cheese, **mozzarella** & rosemary oil

SERVES 4

1 red sweet pepper
1/3 cup olive oil
1 zucchini, thickly sliced
1 globe artichoke bottom, cooked &
  cut into quarters
8 small, flat mushrooms, stems
  removed
1/4 cup tomato purée
12 cherry tomatoes, cut in half
1/2 cup goat cheese, cut
  into 1/2-inch cubes
1/2 cup mozzarella cheese, cut
  into 1/2-inch cubes
Salt & freshly ground black pepper

For the dough
2 teaspoons active dry yeast
1 1/4 cups water
4 cups all-purpose flour
1 teaspoon salt
2 tablespoons olive oil

For the rosemary oil
1 garlic clove, minced
2 tablespoons chopped fresh
  rosemary
1/3 cup extra-virgin olive oil

For the dough, dissolve the yeast in a little of the water. Sift the flour and salt into a bowl and make a well in the center. Pour the yeast liquid into the well with the remaining water and the olive oil and bring it all together with your hands to form a pliable dough. Knead on a lightly floured surface for 6–8 minutes, until smooth and elastic. Place the dough in a lightly oiled bowl, cover with a damp cloth, and let rest at warm room temperature for 1 hour or until doubled in size.

Meanwhile prepare the topping. Preheat the oven to 350°F. Brush the red pepper with a little of the olive oil, place in a baking dish, and roast for 20 minutes. Add the remaining oil to the dish and put the zucchini, artichoke, and mushrooms in it. Season with salt and pepper and return to the oven to roast for about 25 minutes or until all the vegetables are tender. Remove and let cool. Peel the pepper, cut it in half, and remove the seeds. Cut the flesh into strips and set aside.

For the rosemary oil, blitz together the garlic and rosemary with the oil in a blender and set aside.

Raise the oven temperature to 400°F. Punch down the dough, divide it into 4 pieces and roll out each one into a 7-inch disk (or if you're in a party mood, make one big pizza). Spread one quarter of the tomato purée over each pizza base, then top with the roasted vegetables and the halved cherry tomatoes. Scatter both cheeses over the vegetables and drizzle the rosemary oil over. Bake for 15–20 minutes, until golden, then serve immediately.

Dolcelatte and chorizo, a spicy Spanish sausage, make a delicious combination. Add the saltiness and soft texture of oysters and you have a creative and full-flavored pizza.

oyster & spinach pizza with chorizo sausage & melting **dolcelatte**

SERVES 4

6 tablespoons olive oil
2 red onions, thinly sliced
1 pound fresh spinach, washed
16 fresh oysters, shucked (see Tip on page 30)
1 quantity of risen pizza dough (see page 91)
8–9 ounces Spanish chorizo sausage, thinly sliced
3/4 cup crumbled dolcelatte cheese
Salt & freshly ground black pepper

Alternative cheeses
Replace the dolcelatte with some shaved pecorino or Gruyère or grated goat cheese like Rouliabiac or Duddleswell

Preheat the oven to 400°F. Heat 2 tablespoons of the oil in a pan, add the onions, and fry for 10–12 minutes, until lightly golden. Season and remove from the pan. Heat half the remaining oil in the pan, add the spinach, and cook for 2–3 minutes, until wilted. Season with salt and pepper and remove from the pan. Finally, add the rest of the oil to the pan and sauté the oysters for about 1 minute, just enough to seal them. Season and set aside.

Punch down the pizza dough and roll out into four 7-inch disks as in the preceding recipe. Distribute the spinach evenly over the pizza bases. Arrange slices of chorizo on top, then dice the oysters and scatter them over. Scatter the red onions on top and, lastly, the crumbled dolcelatte. Bake for 15 minutes or until the cheese is melted and bubbly. Serve immediately.

These little rice fritters are a speciality of Campania, where they are made with mozzarella and known as suppli al telefono, meaning telephone wires, because the molten cheese forms long strings when the fritters are cut open. My version is made with basil and creamy Gorgonzola, so you don't get the stringy effect of the cheese but you do get a wonderful, melting blue cheese fondue in the center. Serve on a pool of tomato sauce.

suppli alla **gorgonzola** con basilico

SERVES 4

4 tablespoons olive oil
1 onion, finely chopped
1 garlic clove, minced
1 heaped cup Arborio rice
2¼ cups Chicken Stock or Cheese-infused Chicken Stock (see page 16)
4 tablespoons unsalted butter
¾ cup freshly grated Parmesan
A good handful of fresh basil leaves
Freshly grated nutmeg
3 ounces Gorgonzola cheese
3 tablespoons all-purpose flour
2 eggs, beaten
2 cups fresh white bread crumbs
Vegetable oil for deep-frying
Salt & freshly ground black pepper

Heat half the olive oil in a heavy-based pan, add the onion and garlic, and cook over a gentle heat until tender but not browned. Add the rice and stir well. Heat the stock to simmering point in a separate pan. Add a little of the stock to the rice and stir until it has been absorbed. Keep adding the stock, a ladleful at a time, stirring constantly, until the rice is tender but still firm to the bite. Stir in the butter and Parmesan, then spread the mixture out in a large baking pan and let cool.

Put the basil leaves in a blender (reserving a few to garnish the finished dish), add the remaining olive oil, and blitz to a thickish purée. Stir the purée into the cooled rice. Season to taste with nutmeg, salt and pepper, and chill for at least 2 hours, preferably overnight.

To make the suppli, shape the rice mixture into 12–16 balls. Then cut the Gorgonzola into 12–16 pieces and push a piece into the center of each rice ball. Re-form them neatly, pulling the rice back over the cheese and making sure it is completely enclosed. Coat the rice balls in the flour, then in the beaten egg and, finally, in the bread crumbs.

Heat the vegetable oil in a deep fryer or a deep saucepan and fry the suppli in batches for 2–3 minutes, until golden. Drain well on paper towels and then serve immediately, garnished with the reserved basil.

PG TIPS
Suppli can also be made with plain boiled rice and can be stuffed with a variety of fillings, one of my favorites being a mixture of sautéed chicken livers, prosciutto, and wild mushrooms. For a vegetarian option, try sun-dried tomatoes and sautéed eggplant and, of course, use vegetable stock instead.

Fonduta is one of Italy's great classic sauces and I use it a lot with pasta and vegetables. Here it makes a creamy addition to an asparagus risotto. Lightly sautéed wild mushrooms can be stirred into the risotto with the asparagus for added flavor, if desired.

asparagus risotto with **fonduta**

SERVES 4

16 asparagus spears, peeled & well trimmed
9 tablespoons unsalted butter
2 shallots, minced
1 heaped cup Arborio rice
2$^{1}/_{2}$ cups Cheese-infused Chicken Stock (see page 17)
$^{1}/_{3}$ cup dry white wine
Salt & freshly ground black pepper

For the fonduta
7 ounces fontina cheese, rind removed, thinly sliced
5 tablespoons milk
1 tablespoon unsalted butter
2 egg yolks
1$^{1}/_{2}$ tablespoons double cream

Alternative cheeses
Beaufort, Jarlsberg, Gruyère, Emmenthal, or Berkswell

For the fonduta, put the cheese in a pan with the milk and leave for 2 hours.

Meanwhile, cook the asparagus in boiling salted water for 5 minutes or until just tender. Drain, refresh in cold water, and then dry. Cut into thin diagonal slices and set aside.

Put the butter for the fonduta in a stainless steel or glass bowl set over a pan of gently simmering water, making sure the water does not touch the base of the bowl. When it has melted, add the milk-soaked cheese. Stir until the cheese has melted and the mixture has become more solid. Stir in the egg yolks, one at a time. At this stage the mixture will become runny again. Stir constantly until the sauce has thickened, making sure it does not become too hot, otherwise it will curdle. Add the cream and keep warm.

For the risotto, melt 8 tablespoons of the butter in a saucepan, add the shallots, and cook gently until softened but not browned. Add the rice and stir until coated with the butter. Heat the stock to simmering point in a separate pan. Add the white wine and a little of the stock to the rice and stir until the liquid has been absorbed. Keep adding the stock, a ladleful at a time, stirring constantly, until the rice is tender but still retains a bite. Towards the end of cooking, add the stock in smaller quantities and check if the rice is done. It should take about 25 minutes in all.

Add enough of the fonduta to the risotto to give a loose but not sloppy consistency. Melt the remaining butter in a pan and quickly reheat the asparagus in it. Stir the asparagus into the risotto and adjust the seasoning. Divide between 4 serving plates. Serve immediately.

PG TIPS
I like asparagus to be well trimmed before cooking. Snap off the white woody part from the base of each spear, then peel away the skin from the base to the bud at the tip. The older and coarser the asparagus, the more trimming it will need.

This is a very good way of using up leftover risotto and in fact it is worth making extra just for this. A crispy fried risotto cake, it makes an ideal accompaniment to a classic osso buco in a rich tomato sauce, or you can serve it with grilled vegetables for a vegetarian dish.

crispy **cheese** risotto al salto

SERVES 4

2 cups leftover risotto
1/4 cup freshly grated Parmesan
1/2 cup grated fontina or Emmenthal
3 tablespoons vegetable oil
1 tablespoon unsalted butter, melted
Salt & freshly ground black pepper

Mix the cooked risotto with both cheeses and season well with salt and pepper. Heat a heavy-based frying pan over a high heat. Add the oil and then the rice and cheese mixture, packing it down well to form a cake about 1/2–3/4 inch thick. Reduce the heat and cook for about 5 minutes, until golden and crisp around the edges. Turn the cake over and cook for a further 5 minutes, until golden and crispy. Turn out on to a serving dish, brush with the melted butter, and serve cut into wedges.

Walnuts and nutty-flavored Gruyère are a great combination and this makes an excellent dish for autumn. For a real treat, sauté some fresh cèpes with garlic and parsley, then put them on top of the poached gnocchi before adding the two cheeses.

baked walnut gnocchi with **asiago** & **gruyère**

SERVES 4

12 ounces boiling potatoes (preferably King Edward or Maris Piper), peeled & cut into chunks
3/4 cup ground walnuts
3/4 cup grated Asiago cheese
1 tablespoon unsalted butter
2 egg yolks
Scant 1 cup all-purpose flour
Freshly grated nutmeg
Salt & freshly ground black pepper

For the topping
4 tablespoons unsalted butter
1 tablespoon roughly chopped fresh flat-leaf parsley
1/2 cup grated Gruyère cheese
1/4 cup grated Asiago cheese

Cook the potatoes in boiling salted water until tender, then drain well. Mash them while they are still hot. Add the walnuts and Asiago and beat well to help the cheese to melt. Mix in the butter, egg yolks, and half the flour, then season with nutmeg, salt and pepper. Turn the mixture out on to a lightly floured work surface and knead in the remaining flour, a little at a time, to form a smooth, soft but not sloppy dough. Let cool.

Roll out the dough into long cylinders 1 inch thick and cut them into 3/4 inch lengths. Roll each piece over the prongs of a fork to form the classic ridged and slightly curved gnocchi shape. Place the gnocchi on a floured baking sheet and let them dry for about 1 hour.

Preheat the oven to 350°F. Poach the gnocchi, a few at a time, in a large pan of boiling salted water until they rise to the surface, about 2–3 minutes. Remove with a slotted spoon and arrange in a lightly greased, shallow, baking dish.

For the topping, melt the butter and pour it over the gnocchi, then sprinkle them with the parsley, Gruyère, and Asiago. Bake for 12–15 minutes or until the top is brown and crisp. Serve while still bubbling.

The original recipe for these little gnocchi calls for sliced fresh Piedmont truffles–delicious but so expensive! Replace them with white truffle oil which is reasonably priced in comparison and available from specialty food shops. If you do happen to get hold of a white truffle, grate it over the top. Malfattini means misshapen, which is appropriate as these are not the usual gnocchi shape. The sauce is a variation of the classic fonduta (see page 96) but uses pecorino instead of fontina.

malfattini of **ricotta** & arugula with **pecorino** & white truffle oil sauce

SERVES 4

2 tablespoons unsalted butter
6 ounces arugula, plus a few leaves
  to garnish
1³/₄ cups ricotta, sieved
1 cup all-purpose flour
2 eggs
1 egg yolk
1 cup freshly grated Parmesan,
  plus extra to serve
Freshly grated nutmeg
Salt & freshly ground black pepper

For the sauce
1¹/₄ cup coarsely grated pecorino
  Sardo cheese
4 tablespoons unsalted butter
¹/₄ cup mascarpone
²/₃ cup milk
2 tablespoons white truffle oil

Heat the butter in a pan, add the arugula and cook for 1 minute, until wilted. Leave to cool and then mince.

Put the ricotta, flour, eggs and egg yolk in a bowl and mix well together. Stir in the Parmesan and arugula and season with nutmeg, salt and pepper. Shape the mixture into ovals with 2 wet tablespoons, turning it between them. Drop them in batches into a large pan of lightly simmering salted water and cook until they rise to the surface. Remove with a slotted spoon and drain on paper towels. Keep them warm while you make the sauce.

Put the pecorino, butter, mascarpone, and milk in a bowl set over a pan of simmering water, making sure the water isn't touching the base of the bowl. Let the cheese melt slowly, whisking occasionally, then whisk in the truffle oil until the mixture comes together into a sauce. Season to taste.

To serve, warm the malfattini through in a low oven for a couple of minutes if necessary, then arrange them in serving bowls. Pour the sauce over, garnish with arugula, and sprinkle with a little extra Parmesan.

chapter 5 fish, poultry, meat and game

A simple dish with fresh summer flavors. Caprese is the name given to the famous Italian salad of mozzarella, tomato and basil. Here the tomato and cheese serve as a bed for red mullet, which is scattered liberally with fresh basil leaves. (See the photograph on page 2.)

red mullet on baked salad **caprese** with basil & olive oil

SERVES 4

2 balls of cow's milk mozzarella, cut
 into slices $1/2$ inch thick
8 plum tomatoes, skinned & cut into
 slices $1/2$ inch thick
4 x 6-ounce red mullet fillets,
 skin on
A small bunch of fresh basil
$2/3$ cup extra-virgin olive oil
Salt & freshly ground black pepper

Preheat the oven to 425°F. Lightly oil a shallow baking dish large enough to hold the red mullet fillets in a single layer. Arrange overlapping alternate slices of mozzarella and tomato on the bottom of the dish and season with salt and pepper. Lay the mullet fillets on top, skin-side up, season, scatter the basil leaves over, and pour on the olive oil. Bake for 8–10 minutes and then serve immediately.

PG TIPS

I like to serve this dish with some buttery noodles. Sometimes I vary it by adding some diced black olives to the pasta, or even a few sun-dried tomatoes.

Any firm fish would be suitable for this dish. You need to grill the vegetables with the thyme a day in advance and leave them overnight so that their juices run. The juices are then mixed with balsamic vinegar, making a delicious, thyme-scented vinaigrette to drizzle over the fish.

parmesan-crusted sea bass with thyme-grilled vegetables

SERVES 4

3/4 cup freshly grated Parmesan
1/2 cup fresh white bread crumbs
Grated zest of 1/2 lemon
4 x 6-ounce sea bass fillets, skin on
2 eggs, beaten
1/4 cup vegetable oil
2 tablespoons unsalted butter
Salt & freshly ground black pepper

For the vegetables
8 ounces zucchini, cut into
   slices 1/4 inch thick
12 asparagus spears, peeled & well
   trimmed
2 cooked globe artichoke bottoms,
   cut into quarters
1 tablespoon fresh thyme leaves
1/4 cup olive oil
2 tablespoons aged balsamic vinegar

Put the zucchini, asparagus, and cooked artichokes in a roasting pan, season, then sprinkle over the thyme leaves, and toss with the olive oil. Grill over charcoal (or cook under the broiler) for about 5–6 minutes, until the vegetables are slightly charred all over but still retain a bite. Leave overnight in the refrigerator, covered with plastic wrap.

The next day, drain the juices from the vegetables and reserve. Preheat the oven to 350°F.

Mix together the Parmesan, breadcrumbs, lemon zest, and some seasoning. Season the bass fillets on both sides with salt and pepper. Put the beaten eggs in a shallow dish and dip the fish in them to coat both sides, then dip the fish in the Parmesan mixture, pressing it on well.

Reheat the grilled vegetables in the oven. Whisk 3 tablespoons of the reserved cooking juices with the balsamic vinegar.

Heat the oil and butter in a large frying pan until foaming, then add the Parmesan-coated fish fillets. Cook for about 3–4 minutes per side, until golden and crisp. To serve, arrange the thyme-grilled vegetables on serving plates, top with the bass, and drizzle around the vinaigrette.

PG TIPS
For variation, rosemary and oregano could replace the thyme, while other good grilling vegetables such as sweet peppers and eggplants could be substituted for the zucchini, asparagus, and artichokes. Aged balsamic vinegar is best.

Beurre d'escargot tastes so good that it seems a shame to reserve it for serving with snails. Here it is poured over grilled cod, served on a meltingly rich potato and cheese purée. The smell when it hits the table is something else! I like to accompany this dish with some haricots verts or broiled leeks.

saffron-grilled cod fillet with aligot & **beurre d'escargot**

SERVES 4

¼ cup olive oil
1 tablespoon lemon juice
¼ teaspoon saffron strands
4 x 5-ounce cod fillets, skin on
1 quantity of freshly prepared Aligot
(see page 135)
Salt & freshly ground black pepper

For the beurre d'escargot
10 tablespoons unsalted butter
2 garlic cloves, minced
3 tablespoons chopped fresh flat-
leaf parsley, plus a few sprigs
to garnish
¼ teaspoon Dijon mustard
2 tablespoons lemon juice

Put the olive oil, lemon juice and saffron in a pan and warm through to infuse the flavors. Pour this over the cod fillets and leave to marinate, either for 2 hours at room temperature or overnight in the refrigerator.

Next prepare the butter, which can be done well ahead of time. Melt the butter over a low heat, then add the garlic. Raise the heat a little and lightly fry the garlic without letting it color. Stir in the chopped parsley and mustard, then pour into a bowl and let cool. Add the lemon juice and season to taste.

To cook the cod, remove it from the marinade, season well, and place on a ridged cast-iron grill pan (or under the broiler). Cook until tender and golden, about 3–4 minutes per side on a grill pan or 5–6 minutes per side under the broiler. (You could also fry the fish.)

To serve, put a large dollop of aligot on each serving plate and top with the cod. Reheat the parsley and garlic butter and pour it over the fish, then garnish with sprigs of parsley.

PG TIPS
Another way to serve the fish is to cook it lightly as usual, then to top it with a light mixture of fresh breadcrumbs, mustard, and butter and brown it under the broiler before setting it down on the aligot.

This dish calls for the skate to be enclosed in crépinette (pig's caul), which seals in the filling and keeps the fish moist. A good butcher should be able to get it for you. You will need 4 very thin pieces.

wing of skate with **camembert**, spinach, lardons & cider

SERVES 4

4 ounces slab bacon, rind removed,
 cut into 1/4-inch dice
2 cups button mushrooms,
 cut into 1/4-inch dice
4 tablespoons crème fraîche
1 pound spinach, washed
1/2 small Camembert, cut into
 1/4-inch dice
4 x 11-ounch skate wings
4 pieces of crépinette, about
 10 inches square
5 tablespoons dry cider
2/3 cup dry white wine
2/3 cup Chicken Stock (see page 16)
3 tablespoons unsalted butter,
 chilled & diced, plus a little melted
 butter for brushing
2 tablespoons olive oil
1 tablespoon wholegrain mustard
Salt & freshly ground black pepper

Alternative cheese
Cooleeney, sometimes known as
Irish Camembert, or Celtic Promise

Preheat the oven to 400°F. Heat a frying pan until smoking, add the bacon lardons and fry over a high heat until crisp. Add the mushrooms and fry for 2 minutes. Stir in the crème fraîche and cook until reduced by half. Then stir in the spinach, remove from the heat and let cool. Add the diced Camembert and some seasoning.

Coat each skate wing with the Camembert and spinach mixture, spreading it evenly with a metal spatula. Brush the pieces of crépinette with melted butter, then put the skate on them, stuffing-side down. Wrap the fish well in the crépinette and put it in a baking dish large enough to hold it in a single layer. Pour the cider, wine, and chicken stock around the skate. Bake for 12–15 minutes, until tender. Remove the fish and keep warm. Strain the juices into a clean pan and whisk in the diced butter and olive oil a little at a time to form a sauce. Stir in the mustard and adjust the seasoning. Arrange the skate wings on a serving dish, pour over the sauce and serve.

PG TIPS
Other white-fleshed fish such as brill or turbot could replace the skate. Swiss chard or even finely shredded cabbage are good alternatives to the spinach.

Made to a traditional Welsh Caerphilly recipe, which had all but disappeared, it is a wonderful cheese with the crumbly characteristics we have come to know and love. It is very versatile for cooking and here is one of my favorite ways to enjoy a Caerphilly cheese.

braised halibut with **four corners caerphilly** crust, spinach & tomatoes

SERVES 4

4 x 5¹/₂-ounce skinless & boneless
 halibut fillets
¹/₂ cup fish stock
¹/₄ cup dry white wine
6 ounces plum tomatoes, cut
 into quarters (³/₄ cup)
1 tablespoon olive oil
2 tablespoons Dijon mustard
2 tablespoons unsalted butter
1 pound fresh spinach leaves

For the cheese crust
3 ounces fresh white bread crumbs
¹/₂ cup finely grated Four Corners or
 Gorwydd Caerphilly cheese
4 tablespoons unsalted butter,
 softened
4 tablespoons chopped fresh
 basil leaves
2 tablespoons chopped fresh
 tarragon leaves

Alternative cheeses
Cheddar or Emmental

For the crust, place all the ingredients together in a blender and blend until smooth. Spread the mixture out onto a baking sheet lined with plastic wrap and press down so that there are no gaps. Place in the fridge for about 30 minutes to set .

Preheat the oven to 400°F. Place the halibut fillets in a large baking pan. Pour the white wine and fish stock over and season well with salt and pepper. Brush the top of the fish liberally with mustard.

Cut the cheese crust into 4 to fit the top of each fish and lay on top of the fillets. Place in the hot oven, uncovered, and cook for 7–8 minutes or until cooked through.

Meanwhile, heat the butter in a frying pan, add the tomatoes and spinach, and sauté for 2 minutes until wilted. Season to taste.

Place a pile of the spinach and tomato mixture on 4 individual serving plates, top each with the cheese-crusted halibut and serve.

PG TIPS
New potatoes make a lovely, simple accompaniment, but I often like to serve with some creamy oven-baked gratin potatoes.

Sardines have become newly fashionable over the past few years, and, what's more, they're good for us and very reasonably priced. This Parmesan, fennel, and lemon stuffing goes nicely with them. Mackerel can be used instead of sardines, if you prefer.

stuffed sardines with **parmesan** gremolata & caper butter

SERVES 4

24 fresh sardines, about 6 inches
   long, scaled
4 tablespoons olive oil
2 garlic cloves, crushed
1 fennel bulb, with its green feathery
   leaves, finely chopped
1 tablespoon chopped fresh thyme
1 tablespoon chopped fresh oregano
Zest of 1 lemon
1 tablespoon Pernod or other
   aniseed liqueur
1/2 cup fresh white bread crumbs
1/2 cup Parmesan, freshly grated
Freshly grated nutmeg
Salt & freshly ground black pepper

For the caper butter
5 tablespoons unsalted butter
2 shallots, minced
3 tablespoons capers,
   rinsed & drained
1 tablespoon chopped fresh parsley
Juice of 1 lemon

Alternative cheeses
"Dry Aged Jack", Grana padana (a
cheaper version of Parmesan),
Asiago, pecorino

Preheat the oven to 400°F. Slit the sardines open along the belly and carefully pull out the entrails. Open the fish flat and carefully pull out the backbone from the head to the tail, snipping it off at the tail end with scissors and leaving the head and tail intact. Set the fish aside.

Heat half the oil in a pan, add the garlic, and cook gently until tender. Add the fennel and cook for 5 minutes. Then stir in the herbs, lemon zest, and Pernod, followed by the bread crumbs and Parmesan. Season to taste with nutmeg, salt and pepper and remove from the heat.

Fill the cavity of each sardine with this mixture, pressing it in well. Put the fish on an oiled baking sheet, brush them with the remaining oil and bake for 8–10 minutes, until cooked through.

For the caper butter, melt the butter over a low heat, then add the shallots, capers, and parsley. Cook until the butter begins to foam and becomes nutty in fragrance. Add the lemon juice, then immediately pour the butter over the sardines and serve.

This is based on that great dish, lobster Thermidor. All you need to serve with it is a simple rice pilaff.

gratin of lobster with **parmesan** & tarragon sauce

SERVES 4

4 cooked lobsters, weighing about 1 pound
2 tablespoons unsalted butter
Cayenne pepper, to taste
5 tablespoons dry white wine
1 tablespoon chopped fresh tarragon, plus a few sprigs to garnish
1¼ cups Basic Cheese Sauce (see page 18)
¼ cup heavy cream, semi-whipped
3 tablespoons freshly grated Parmesan
Salt & freshly ground black pepper

Cut the claws off the lobster with a large knife, then split the lobster in half down the back: the easiest way to do this is to put a large knife through the center of the body section and cut down through the head, then take out the knife, turn the lobster around and cut down the center of the body through the tail. Remove and discard the head sac and the intestinal vein, then take out the lobster meat from the head and tail and cut it into large cubes. Discard the gills (known as "dead men's fingers") from the lobster shells and reserve the shells. Crack the claws in 2 or 3 places and pick out the meat.

Heat the butter in a pan, add the lobster meat, and season with salt, pepper, and cayenne. Pour in the white wine, bring to a boil, and simmer for 1 minute—no longer or the lobster will toughen. Remove the lobster from the pan with a slotted spoon and continue to boil the wine until it is reduced by half its original volume. Stir in the chopped tarragon and the cheese sauce, then fold in the cream. Return the lobster to the pan. Adjust the seasoning.

Fill the 8 lobster shells with the lobster mixture and put them on a baking sheet or in a shallow gratin dish. Sprinkle with the grated Parmesan. Brown under the broiler and then serve, garnished with sprigs of tarragon.

Manchego is Spain's best-known cheese and, when fresh, has a mild, creamy consistency. Many Spanish recipes begin with instructions to prepare a sofrito–onions, garlic, tomatoes and sometimes parsley, cooked slowly to make a thick, intensely flavored savory base. This particular dish is of Mexican-Spanish origin and could be made with almost any seafood. Try lobster or scallops for an extravagant version. Saffron rice makes a good accompaniment.

sizzling prawns with sofrito, peppers & **manchego**

SERVES 4

1/4 cup olive oil
4 tablespoons unsalted butter
2 garlic cloves, minced
20–24 large raw prawns, peeled &
  deveined
1 red onion, cut into wedges about
  1/4 inch thick
2 red sweet peppers, seeded
  & cut into strips 1/2 inch wide
1 green sweet pepper, seeded &
  cut into strips 1/2 inch wide
12 ounces tomatoes, skinned,
  seeded & chopped (about 11/2 cups)
A pinch of cayenne pepper
1/2 teaspoon paprika
9 ounces Manchego cheese, cut into
  3/4 inch cubes (about 1 heaped cup)
2 tablespoons fresh cilantro leaves
Salt & freshly ground black pepper

Alternative cheese
Feta or "Dry Aged Jack"

Heat the oil and butter in a frying pan until the butter is foaming, then add the garlic and cook for 1 minute. Throw in the prawns and sauté them over a fairly high heat for about 1–2 minutes, until colored. Remove from the pan and keep warm. Add the onion and peppers to the pan, cover, and cook over a low heat for 15 minutes, until softened.

Stir in the tomatoes, cayenne, and paprika and cook for about 5 minutes, until the tomatoes begin to break down. Return the prawns to the pan, and stir together, then add the Manchego and sauté for 30 seconds. Season to taste, scatter the fresh cilantro over and serve immediately.

I think that it's fair to say that most cheese dishes simply include a little cheese rather than use it as the main ingredient. One exception is fondue, a dish invented in the Swiss Alps to use the famous cheeses of the region, Emmenthal and Gruyère. My favorite fondue combines Emmenthal with Camembert from Normandy for a tasty modern variation. It is very important to have a proper fondue pot. This is easy to find and well worth a small investment in order to keep your fondue at the right temperature.

mussel **fondue** normandie

**SERVES 6 AS AN APPETIZER,
4 AS A MAIN COURSE**

2 cups grated Emmenthal cheese
1 tablespoon cornstarch
1/2 garlic clove
1 1/2 cups dry white wine
9 ounces very ripe Camembert
   cheese, rind removed,
   cut into small pieces
6 tablespoons dry hard cider
Freshly grated nutmeg
Salt & freshly ground black pepper

For the mussels
2 pounds fresh mussels
1 shallot, minced
A few parsley stems
3/4 cup dry white wine

First clean the mussels. Scrub them under cold running water, pulling out their "beards" and scraping off any barnacles with a knife. Discard any open mussels that do not close when tapped lightly on a work surface.

For the fondue, gently toss the Emmenthal with the cornstarch and set aside. Rub the inside of a fondue pot or earthenware casserole with the cut surface of the garlic. Pour in the white wine and cook over a low heat until it just starts to bubble. Gradually stir in the Emmenthal and keep stirring until smooth. Then add the Camembert and blend together until the Camembert melts and the mixture is smooth again. Add the cider, and season with salt, pepper, and nutmeg. Keep warm.

Place the mussels in a pan with the shallot, parsley stems, and white wine. Cover with a tight-fitting lid and cook over a high heat, shaking the pan once or twice, until the mussels have opened (about 3–4 minutes). Drain them in a colander, reserving the cooking liquid, and discard any mussels that remain closed. Remove the mussels from their shells and keep warm. Strain the cooking liquid and add to the fondue. Serve the mussels with fondue forks to dip into the Camembert fondue.

PG TIPS
Any seafood would be good instead of mussels. I sometimes serve the fondue with new potatoes: dip them into the pot too–delicious!

The classic combination of mozzarella, tomato, and basil in a different guise. You can use turbot or a similar white fish instead of chicken and it works just as well. Tomato tapenade is now available in jars in many supermarkets, but I still think that home-made is better. Besides, it's really quick to make your own. You won't need to use all of it in this recipe, but it keeps well in the refrigerator.

chicken schnitzel with **mozzarella**, tomato tapenade & basil

SERVES 4

4 x 5-ounce skinless & boneless
  chicken breasts
Flour, for dusting
1 egg, beaten
$1/4$ cup fresh white bread crumbs
$1/4$ cup olive oil
$1/2$ cup unsalted butter
1 ball of mozzarella, cut into 8 slices
2 tablespoons roughly chopped
  fresh basil
Juice of $1/2$ lemon
Salt & freshly ground black pepper

For the tomato tapenade
$1 1/2$ cups sun-dried tomatoes
$2 1/2$ tablespoons capers, rinsed
  & drained
2 garlic cloves, minced
$1/4$ cup oil from the sun-dried
  tomatoes

For the tapenade, put all the ingredients in a blender and blitz to a coarse purée (do not process it too finely or it will become mushy).

Put the chicken breasts between 2 sheets of plastic wrap and beat lightly with a meat pounder or the end of a rolling pin until they are just under $1/4$ inch thick. Season with salt and pepper, then dust lightly with flour. Dip them in the beaten egg and then in the bread crumbs. Brush off any excess crumbs.

Heat the olive oil and 2 tablespoons of the butter in a frying pan and add the chicken. Cook for about 4–5 minutes on each side, until the chicken is golden and cooked through, then transfer to heatproof serving plates. Top each chicken breast with 2 slices of mozzarella, then spread $1/2$ tablespoon of tomato tapenade over the cheese. Place under the broiler until the mozzarella begins to soften.

Meanwhile, heat the remaining butter in a frying pan until it is foaming and smells nutty. Add the basil and lemon juice, pour it over the chicken and serve immediately.

PG TIPS
Sometimes I make this with tomato tapenade spread over one slice of mozzarella and black olive tapenade on the other. The contrast of black, red and white looks spectacular. (Olive tapenade is available in jars in most supermarkets.)

I recently discovered spatchcocked poussins in a major supermarket. What a superb idea! All the work has been done for you. If you are not lucky enough to find them, don't be too alarmed at the thought of preparing the birds yourself. After a few attempts you'll wonder what all the fuss was about. Your guests will be impressed too. Serve the chickens with a watercress salad and new potatoes.

grilled chicken spatchcock with **tomme, ricotta verde & sweet shallot vinaigrette**

SERVES 4

4 x 1 pound poussins, free-range
  if possible
3 ounces white Tomme cheese
Scant 1/2 cup ricotta cheese
1 bunch of watercress, stems
  removed, leaves finely chopped
2 tablespoons chopped fresh basil
1 shallot, minced
1 garlic clove, minced
2 tablespoons olive oil
Lemon wedges, to serve
Salt & freshly ground black pepper

For the marinade
1 garlic clove, minced
Juice & grated zest of 2 lemons
1/4 cup olive oil

For the vinaigrette
4 shallots, finely sliced
1/2 tablespoon unsalted butter
A pinch of sugar
1 tablespoon champagne vinegar
  or white wine vinegar
1/4 cup olive oil
1/2 teaspoon Dijon mustard

To spatchcock the poussins, you simply need to open them out flat. To do this, cut out the backbone with kitchen scissors or poultry shears. Break the wishbone, then turn each bird cut-side down and flatten it by pressing down with the heel of your hand. Turn it over and remove all the ribcage bones.

Mix together all the ingredients for the marinade, season with salt and pepper and pour into a large shallow container–you might need 2 to hold the poussins. Add the poussins, turning them to coat them, cover and let marinate for at least 4 hours, but preferably overnight, in the refrigerator.

To make the vinaigrette, gently fry the shallots in the butter with the sugar until golden and lightly caramelized. Whisk together the vinegar, oil, mustard, and some salt and pepper. Add the hot shallots and let cool. (This can be done several hours in advance.)

In a bowl, mix together the Tomme, ricotta, watercress, basil, shallot, garlic, and olive oil. Season to taste. Remove the poussins from the marinade and dry well. Carefully loosen the skin of each bird without detaching it and push the stuffing underneath, spreading it over the flesh–it's easiest to use your fingers. Smooth the skin over again and season with salt and pepper.

Grill the poussins over charcoal for about 7–8 minutes on each side, until tender and cooked through. A charcoal grill would be ideal but you could use a ridged grill pan instead, or fry them. Put them on warmed serving plates, drizzle a little of the vinaigrette over and serve the rest on the side. Accompany with lemon wedges.

PG TIPS
If you find it difficult removing the ribcage from the raw poussins, take out the bones after the birds have been cooked. They will come away much more easily.

This may seem rather an unusual combination but, if you think about it, grapes are invariably served on a cheeseboard and they are also often cooked with quails. This recipe brings all three ingredients together. Muscat grapes are recommended for their exceptional sweetness, although the dish also works well with red grapes. Serve with artichoke bottoms or haricots verts that have been sautéed in butter with bacon and onions. If you cannot get hold of quails, you could use 4 poussins instead, in which case you would need to double the amount of stuffing.

quails stuffed with **sage derby** & muscat grapes

SERVES 4

8 quails, boned (ask your butcher to do this & give you the bones, if possible)
1/2 cup unsalted softened butter
1 cup grated Sage Derby cheese
1 shallot, minced
1 small garlic clove, minced
Salt & freshly ground black pepper

For the sauce
1/3 cup white wine
1 1/4 cups Reduced Meat Stock (see page 17)
12 ounces muscat grapes
3 tablespoons Muscat de Beaumes de Venise or vin de Jura

Alternative cheeses
Dolcelatte would be ideal. Even a stronger blue, such as Stilton or Roquefort, would work well or you could use a milder Cornish Blue

Preheat the oven to 425°F. Season the quails inside and out. Prepare the stuffing by beating together 6 tablespoons of the butter, the Sage Derby, shallot, garlic, and a little seasoning. Stuff the quails with this mixture and seal them by pulling the skin over the opening and securing with a wooden toothpick. Place in a small roasting pan. Melt the remaining butter and brush it over the quails, then roast for 12–15 minutes, until juicy and tender and still slightly pink. Remove from the roasting pan and keep warm.

For the sauce, put the quail bones in the roasting pan, place it on a medium heat, and fry until the bones are golden brown. Add the white wine and bring to a boil, stirring to scrape up the sediment from the base of the tin. Simmer for 2 minutes, until the wine has evaporated. Pour in the meat stock and bring to a boil, skimming off any impurities from the surface. Reduce the heat and simmer for 10 minutes.

Meanwhile, pass half the grapes through a centrifugal juice extractor. When the sauce has reduced and thickened to a light, syrupy consistency, strain it through a sieve into a clean tin, add the Beaumes de Venise or vin de Jura and the fresh grape juice. Simmer for 2 minutes, then add the remaining grapes to the sauce and reheat until boiling. Adjust the seasoning to taste.

Return the quails to the oven for 2 minutes to reheat them, then put them on 4 serving plates. Pour the sauce around the quails and serve.

PG TIPS
If you do not have a centrifugal juice extractor, purée the grapes in a blender, then sieve the purée. If seedless grapes are unavailable, remove seeds with a clean bobby pin or by cutting the grapes in half and removing the seeds.

I often serve this winter-inspired dish around Christmas time, garnished with roasted baby onions and glazed chestnuts– delicious! Pheasant has a tendency to be dry if not cooked with care. By wrapping the breasts in bacon you can keep them moist and tender.

roast breast of pheasant wrapped in smoked bacon with caraway cabbage & **gorgonzola** polenta

SERVES 4

4 pheasant breasts, bones removed
 & chopped
8 bacon slices
4 tablespoons vegetable oil
6 tablespoons unsalted butter
1 head Savoy cabbage, central core
 removed, finely shredded
1 teaspoon caraway seeds
1¼ cups water
Freshly grated nutmeg
½ quantity of Gorzonzola Polenta
 (see page 132)
Salt & freshly ground black pepper

For the sauce
3 shallots, roughly chopped
1 garlic clove, roughly chopped
1 sprig of fresh thyme
1 bay leaf
6 juniper berries, lightly crushed
6 black peppercorns, lightly crushed
5 tablespoons red wine vinegar
²/₃ cup red wine
²/₃ cup Meat Stock (see page 17)
¼ cup port
¼ cup red currant jelly

Preheat the oven to 425°F. Season the pheasant breasts all over with salt and pepper, then wrap each one in 2 overlapping slices of bacon. Secure with a wooden toothpick. Heat half the oil and butter in an ovenproof frying pan or shallow casserole dish until foaming, then add the pheasant breasts and fry briefly until browned all over. Transfer to the oven and roast for 8–10 minutes, until tender.

Meanwhile, heat the remaining oil in a saucepan and cook the cabbage over a low heat until it begins to wilt. Add the remaining butter, the caraway seeds, and water. Bring to a boil and cook until the cabbage is tender and all the liquid has evaporated. Then season with salt, pepper, and a little nutmeg and keep warm.

Remove the pheasant breasts from the oven and take out the toothpicks. Keep the pheasant warm while you make the sauce. Put the chopped pheasant bones, shallots, garlic, thyme, bay leaf, juniper berries, and peppercorns in the pan in which the pheasant was cooked and fry gently for 2–3 minutes, until golden. Pour in the vinegar and boil for 1 minute, stirring to scrape up the sediment from the bottom of the pan. Add the red wine and boil until the liquid has reduced to half its original volume. Next add the stock and boil until reduced by a third. Stir in the port and red currant jelly and adjust the seasoning. Strain through a fine-mesh strainer.

To serve, reheat the polenta if necessary. Arrange the cabbage on 4 warmed serving plates and place the pheasant on top. Garnish with a large scoop of polenta and pour the sauce around.

This recipe sounds like a contradiction in terms, since the whole point of steak tartare is that it is served raw. But what I've done is taken the ingredients for steak tartare—best-quality ground beef, Worcestershire sauce, onions, capers, mustard, and egg yolk—and put them together into a hamburger, with the added bonus of delicious, melting Roquefort cheese in the center. Serve with good chunky fries and a crisp green salad.

grilled steak tartare with **roquefort**

SERVES 4

1³/₄ pounds ground round or sirloin
2 tablespoons Worcestershire sauce
1 onion, minced
1 tablespoon capers, rinsed,
  drained & chopped
1 tablespoon chopped fresh parsley
1 tablespoon Dijon mustard
1 egg yolk
1 cup crumbled Roquefort cheese
Salt & freshly ground black pepper

Alternative cheeses
For a different flavor entirely,
substitute goat cheese or
Emmenthal for the Roquefort

Mix the beef, Worcestershire sauce, onion, capers, parsley, and mustard together in a bowl. Season with salt and pepper, then mix in the egg yolk. Chill for about 30 minutes, until firm.

Divide the mixture into 4 balls. With your thumb, make an indentation in each one and fill with the Roquefort. Pull the meat back over the cheese until it is completely covered. Flatten into hamburgers, season lightly. Grill over charcoal, or on a cast-iron grill pan, or cook under the broiler.

This is a good dish for outdoor cooking as it can be put together very easily. However, if it rains, you can always grill or fry the steaks indoors.

pepper-crusted rib eye of beef with **roquefort** butter, sautéed potatoes & porcini mushrooms

SERVES 4

1 pound new potatoes
1 cup olive oil
7 ounces fresh porcini mushrooms,
  thinly sliced
2 tablespoons roughly chopped
  fresh sage
4 x 10-ounce beef rib eye steaks,
  well trimmed
2 tablespoons coarsely ground
  black peppercorns
1/2 quantity of Roquefort Butter
  (see page 19)
Salt

Cook the potatoes in boiling salted water until just tender, then drain and leave until cool enough to handle. Peel and cut into slices 1/2 inch thick. Heat the oil in a frying pan, add the potatoes and sauté until golden and tender. Add the porcini and sage and sauté until the mushrooms are tender. Season with salt and pepper and keep warm.

Coat the rib eye steaks evenly with the coarsely ground peppercorns and season with a little salt. Grill over charcoal until done to your liking.

Arrange the potatoes on 4 serving plates, top with the steaks, and put a pat of Roquefort butter on top of each steak. Serve immediately. The delicate cheese butter will melt on its way to the table.

PG TIPS
If you can't get fresh porcini mushrooms, use portabello mushrooms instead. This simple recipe lends itself to many adaptations—for instance, lamb or pork chops, or a rump steak. The cheese butter is an ideal way to use up scraps of cheese.

This dish evolved from the French classic, steak Bordelaise, which is beef in a red wine sauce with beef bone marrow. In my adaptation the marrow is topped with shaved Parmesan and the sauce enriched with aged balsamic vinegar. I generally serve it with buttered spinach with fresh porcini mushrooms and pan-roasted shallots alongside, but any green vegetable would be good.

filet of beef with bone marrow & **parmesan** crostini & red wine balsamic vinegar jus

SERVES 4

4 x 6-ounch filet steaks, well trimmed (cut the trimmings into small pieces & save for the sauce)
3 tablespoons vegetable oil
1 cup finely diced mixed vegetables, such as onion, leek & carrot,
1 cup red wine
1/4 cup aged balsamic vinegar
1 1/4 cups Reduced Meat Stock (see page 17)
8 large slices of beef bone marrow (see Tip)
4 round bread croûtes, 3 inches in diameter, toasted
1 ounce fresh Parmesan, cut into shavings
Salt & freshly ground black pepper

Alternative cheese
Asiago

Season the steaks with salt and pepper. Heat the oil in a large heavy-based frying pan until smoking. Fry the steaks quickly on both sides so that they turn a beautiful rich dark color, then cook until they are done to your liking: 2–3 minutes per side for rare, 5–6 for medium. Remove from the pan and keep warm in a low oven. Add the meat trimmings to the pan, along with the mixed vegetables, and fry until golden. Pour in the red wine and balsamic vinegar and bring to a boil, stirring to scrape up the sediment from the bottom of the pan. Boil for 5 minutes, then pour in the stock and simmer until it has thickened slightly and become syrupy; it should be thick enough to coat the back of a spoon. Taste and adjust the seasoning if necessary.

Meanwhile, poach the slices of marrow in a little salted water or, better still, meat stock for 1 minute, then drain. Put 2 slices of poached marrow on each croûte and cover with the shaved Parmesan. Put the steaks on warm serving plates, top each one with a marrow crostini and pour the red wine sauce around. Grind some black pepper over the top and serve.

PG TIPS
You will have to go to a good old-fashioned butcher's shop to get bone marrow. A very co-operative butcher might extract the marrow from the bone for you. If not, ask for bones cut into 3-inch lengths and then poach them for 1–2 minutes. This will enable you to scoop out the marrow easily.

A cheese rarebit is a peculiarly English dish that dates back at least to the time of Shakespeare. I came across this 18th-century recipe for blue cheese rarebit in an old cookery book. I like to make it with one of my favorite cheeses, Scottish Dunsyre Blue.

veal steaks with **blue cheese** rarebit, roasted celery root & rosemary sauce

SERVES 4

1$1/2$ pounds celery root, peeled &
  cut into sticks 4 inches long and
  $3/4$ inch thick
$1/3$ cup vegetable oil
7 ounces finely diced Dunsyre Blue
  (about 1$1/2$ cups)
2 teaspoons Dijon mustard
$1/2$ cup light beer
4 x 5-ounce veal tenderloin steaks
  (or veal chops)
Salt & freshly ground black pepper

For the sauce
2 tablespoons unsalted butter
2 shallots, minced
1 tablespoon chopped fresh
  rosemary
$2/3$ cup red wine
2 cups Reduced Meat Stock
  (see page 17)

Alternative cheeses
Any blue such as Stilton,
Beenleigh Blue, Bleu des Causses
or Y-Fenni

Preheat the oven to 400°F. Blanch the celery root in boiling salted water for 2–3 minutes, then drain well in a colander. Place on a baking sheet, toss with half the oil, and bake for 20–25 minutes, until golden.

Meanwhile, for the rarebit, put the cheese, mustard, and beer in a pan over a low heat and cook, stirring constantly, until the cheese melts; the mixture should be the consistency of thickish cream. Season with pepper and keep warm.

Heat the remaining oil in a frying pan, season the veal steaks and fry for about 3–5 minutes on each side. Remove from the pan and keep warm.

For the sauce, add the butter, shallots, and rosemary to the pan in which the veal was cooked and fry until the shallots are lightly golden. Pour in the red wine and boil for 2–3 minutes, then add the meat stock. Boil until reduced and thickened to a saucelike consistency, then strain through a fine sieve.

Spread the blue cheese rarebit over the veal steaks and place under the broiler for 2–3 minutes, until the rarebit has turned golden and bubbly. Transfer to serving plates, pour the sauce around, and garnish with the roasted celery root.

My new-look saltimbocca uses all the elements of one of Italy's classic dishes, with the addition of thinly sliced fontina and a light Parmesan crust. In spring, asparagus tips and baby leeks make good accompaniments.

new-look **saltimbocca**

SERVES 4

4 x 7-ounce thin veal scallops
4 slices of prosciutto
8 thin slices of fontina cheese,
  rind removed
Flour, for dusting
3 eggs, beaten
3/4 cup freshly grated Parmesan
1 cup fresh white bread crumbs
1/4 cup vegetable oil or
  clarified butter (see Tip on page 83)
2 lemons, peel & pith removed, cut
  into slices 1/4 inch thick
Salt & freshly ground black pepper

For the sauce
1 1/4 cups Reduced Meat Stock
  (see page 17)
1/4 cup Marsala wine
6 tablespoons unsalted butter
20 small fresh sage leaves
2 tablespoons lemon juice

Alternative cheeses
Port Salut or Fontal

The veal scallops should be no more than 1/8 inch thick. If necessary, put them between 2 sheets of plastic wrap and flatten with a meat pounder or a rolling pin. Season the scallops with salt and pepper. Lay a slice of prosciutto on top of each one, then 2 slices of fontina. Fold up the edges of the veal to enclose the filling. Season again, then dust lightly with flour and chill for 30 minutes.

For the sauce, bring the stock and Marsala to a boil and simmer until it forms a light sauce consistency.

Beat together the eggs, Parmesan and breadcrumbs and add a little seasoning. Heat the oil or clarified butter in a large frying pan. Dip each veal scallop into the egg and cheese mixture to coat, then fry for about 5 minutes on each side, until golden and cooked through. Transfer to a warm serving dish, top each scallop with 2 slices of lemon and pour the Marsala sauce around. Heat the butter until it is foaming and gives off a nutty aroma. Add the sage leaves and lemon juice and then pour over the veal. Serve immediately.

PG TIPS
It can be difficult judging the correct consistency of a sauce. If it seems too thin, reduce it by boiling until it has thickened enough to coat the back of a spoon.

A creamy potato purée or some soft or grilled polenta would go well with the grilled lamb and sautéed red sweet peppers in this dish.

chargrilled lamb chops with cilantro & **goat cheese** pesto & peppers

SERVES 4

1/3 cup olive oil
2 garlic cloves, minced
1 small hot red chili pepper
4 red sweet peppers, seeded
1 tablespoon white wine vinegar
8 thickly cut lamb rib chops
1/2 quantity of Cilantro & Goat
  Cheese Pesto (see page 20)
Salt & freshly ground black pepper

Heat the olive oil in a frying pan, add the garlic and the whole chili and cook for 1 minute over a low heat to infuse the oil. Cut the peppers into strips 1/2 inch wide and add to the pan, season with salt and pepper and sauté for 3–4 minutes. Add a little water, cover and cook over a low heat for 10–15 minutes, until tender. Uncover the pan, raise the heat and cook until all the liquid has evaporated. Add the vinegar and cook until that, too, has evaporated. Remove the chili and adjust the seasoning. Keep warm.

Season the lamb chops and grill them over charcoal or on a ridged cast iron grill pan until they are done to your liking. Arrange the peppers on 4 serving plates, top with the lamb chops, spoon the pesto over and serve.

Lamb shanks are always popular because they are tasty and very good value for money. Here they are served with Greek ingredients– oregano, feta, lemon, and olive oil–to make a hearty, satisfying dish.

lamb shanks with **feta**, anchovy & braised chickpeas

SERVES 6

1 tablespoon anchovy fillets, rinsed
2 tablespoons grated lemon zest
2 tablespoons chopped fresh oregano
1/4 cup olive oil
2 garlic cloves, minced
6 small lamb shanks, trimmed
6 ounces Greek feta cheese
Salt & freshly ground black pepper

For the chickpeas
2 tablespoons olive oil
1 onion, minced
1/2 tablespoon ground cumin
1 teaspoon turmeric
1 heaped cup dried chickpeas,
  soaked overnight & then drained
4 tomatoes, skinned & chopped
1 1/4 cups tomato purée

For the chickpeas, heat the oil in a pan, add the onion, cumin, and turmeric and sweat until the onion is tender. Add the chickpeas, cover with water, and bring to a boil. Reduce the heat and simmer for 1 hour, or until the chickpeas are tender. About 10 minutes before the end of cooking, add the chopped tomatoes and purée to form a thick sauce around the chickpeas. Season to taste.

Mince the anchovy fillets and mix together with the lemon zest, oregano, oil and garlic to make a paste. Rub the paste all over the lamb shanks. Leave to marinate for up to 2 hours at room temperature.

Grill the lamb over charcoal or a ridged cast iron grill pan for 10–12 minutes on each side (this gives pink lamb), or until done to your liking.

Meanwhile, reheat the braised chickpeas and arrange on serving plates. Top with the lamb and coarsely grate the feta over the top. Serve immediately.

chapter 6 **vegetable dishes**

Leeks and bacon make a wonderful marriage of flavors. With the addition of Red Leicester cheese, this simple gratin reaches new heights. It makes an ideal accompaniment to a good Sunday roast.

gratin of leeks with **red leicester** & bacon

SERVES 4

A pinch of sugar
8 medium leeks
1 tablespoon unsalted butter
1 tablespoon all-purpose flour
1¼ cups Vegetable Stock (see
  page 16) or low fat milk
1 teaspoon Dijon mustard
⅓ cup heavy cream
1 cup grated Red Leicester
2 ounces (2 slices) bacon, rind
  removed, coarsely chopped
Salt & freshly ground black pepper

Bring a pan of water to a boil with the sugar and some salt. Plunge the leeks into the water and simmer for 8–10 minutes, until just tender. Remove and drain well, then dry on a cloth.

Melt the butter in a pan, stir in the flour, and cook over a gentle heat for 1–2 minutes. Gradually add the stock or milk and bring to a boil, stirring constantly. Reduce the heat and cook very gently for 10 minutes. Remove from the heat and stir in the mustard, cream, and half the cheese, then season to taste. Arrange the leeks in a gratin dish, season, and coat with the sauce.

In a hot frying pan, cook the bacon until crisp. Drain and scatter it over the leeks. Finally, sprinkle over the remaining cheese. Place under the broiler for a few minutes until bubbling and golden. Serve immediately.

I find this creamy blue cheese polenta far superior to the plain variety finished with Parmesan.

soft **gorgonzola** polenta with young spinach & wild mushrooms

SERVES 4–6

2 tablespoons unsalted butter
5 ounces mixed wild mushrooms, such as cépes, chanterelles, & oyster mushrooms, halved if large
1/3 cup Madeira or port
1 1/4 cups Meat Stock (see page 17)
2 tablespoons olive oil (about 1 cup)
4 ounces young spinach leaves, washed
Freshly grated nutmeg
1 tablespoon chopped fresh chives, to garnish
Salt & freshly ground black pepper

For the polenta
2 quarts water
2 teaspoons salt
1/2 cup unsalted butter
2 cups polenta flour
1 heaped cup crumbled Gorgonzola cheese

Alternative cheeses
Bleu de Bresse, Blue Castello (AUS) or Yorkshire Blue

For the polenta, bring the water, salt, and butter to a boil in a large pan. Slowly rain in the polenta, stirring all the time. Simmer over a gentle heat for 30–35 minutes, stirring very frequently, until cooked; the polenta should be pulling away from the sides of the pan. Remove from the heat, stir in the Gorgonzola, and let it to melt. The polenta should be quite soft and smooth in texture. Adjust the seasoning and keep warm.

Heat the butter in a pan and fry the wild mushrooms over a high heat until tender. Remove the mushrooms from the pan and set aside. Pour in the Madeira or port and stock and boil until the liquid has reduced by half. Season to taste, return the mushrooms to the pan and keep warm.

Heat the olive oil in a pan, add the spinach, and cook until just wilted, then season with nutmeg, salt, and pepper.

To serve, pour the polenta into 4 warmed shallow bowls, place the spinach in the center, and arrange the mushrooms on top. Garnish with the chives.

Some people find the idea of cooking a soufflé too daunting to contemplate, but as long as you follow the rules it can be a very simple dish to add to your repertoire. Here is one of my personal favorites. A delicious variation for any cheese soufflé is to put some diced cheese in the center of the mixture when you are filling the dish. It will melt as the soufflé cooks, resulting in a wonderful fondue-like texture.

eggplant & **roquefort** soufflé

SERVES 6

2 tablespoons freshly
  grated Parmesan
1/2 cup olive oil
3 medium eggplants, peeled & cut
  into small cubes
2/3 cup water
A good pinch of paprika
3 ounces Roquefort, crumbled
  (about 1/2 cup)
3 tablespoons unsalted butter, plus
  extra for greasing
1/4 cup all-purpose flour
1 cup milk, boiled & strained
4 egg yolks
6 egg whites
Salt & freshly ground black pepper

Alternative cheeses
**Oregon Blue, Bleu d'Auvergne,
Lanark Blue or Meredith Blue (AUS)**

Butter six 1-cup soufflé dishes or one 5-cup soufflé dish and dust them with the Parmesan, turning the dishes to coat them evenly. Tip out any excess cheese.

Preheat the oven to 450°F. Heat the olive oil in a large frying pan, add the eggplants and fry until lightly golden. Don't crowd the pan: you may have to cook them in batches. Return all the eggplants to the pan, add the water, cover and cook over a gentle heat for up to 30 minutes, stirring occasionally, until the eggplants are very soft and fairly dry in texture. Put them in a blender with a little salt, some pepper, and the paprika. To this add 1/4 cup of the Roquefort and blitz to a smooth, thickish purée. Set aside.

Heat the butter in a pan, add the flour, and cook over a low heat for a few minutes. Gradually add the hot milk, stirring all the time, then bring to a boil to make a smooth sauce. Cook over a very low heat for about 5 minutes, then stir in the eggplant and Roquefort purée. Let cool slightly before stirring in the egg yolks.

Whisk the egg whites until they form stiff peaks. Beat a third of the whites into the sauce to loosen the mixture, then carefully fold in the remaining whites. Half fill the soufflé dishes with the mixture and scatter the remaining Roquefort over the top. Pour over the remaining soufflé mixture and wipe any drips off the rims of the dishes. Place on a baking sheet and bake for 20 minutes, until all the soufflés are well risen and nicely golden.
Serve immediately.

PG TIPS
For successful soufflé making: Ensure that the bowl in which you whisk the egg whites is clean and greasefree; rub it with a little lemon, then rinse under cold water and dry with a clean cloth. Do not overbeat the egg whites or they will become grainy. Be careful not to leave fingerprints along the rim of the soufflé dish or the soufflé will not rise evenly. Soufflés must be served immediately. Remember: "The guests should wait for the soufflé and not the other way round!"

Aligot is a peasant dish from the Auvergne region of France and makes hearty and sustaining cold-weather fare. In some areas garlic is traditionally included. It's very good served with sausages, braised meat, or even, less conventionally, with fish—see the recipe for Saffron-grilled Cod Fillet with Aligot and Beurre d'Escargot on page 104.

aligot (cheese & potato purée)

SERVES 4

2 pounds boiling potatoes
3/4 cup milk, boiled & strained
5 tablespoons heavy cream or
  crème fraîche
4 tablespoons unsalted butter
4 ounces (4 slices) bacon, diced
1 pound full-fat Tomme cheese,
  such as Cantal, cut into
  thin slivers
Salt & freshly ground black pepper

Alternative cheeses
Although Cantal is the usual cheese, Gruyère, Emmenthal, fontina and even Lancashire all make good substitutes

Peel the potatoes and cook them in boiling salted water until tender. Drain well and mash until very smooth, then beat in the milk, cream, or crème fraîche and butter.

In a separate pan, fry the bacon until it is crisp and the fat has been released. Add the fat (not the bacon itself) to the potato purée and season to taste. Place over a low heat and gradually fold in the cheese using a spatula. Beat the mixture; as it becomes elastic it will soften slightly and eventually be stringy when lifted with the spoon. As soon as it reaches this stage, you should serve the dish immediately.

PG TIPS
Aligot loses its heat fairly quickly, therefore your guests must be ready to eat it at once to appreciate it at its best. Vegetarians may omit the bacon fat.

In my adaptation of this classic Italian dish from Campania, the eggplant slices are rolled up with a cheese, basil and raisin stuffing rather than layered in the usual way. It makes a delicious and substantial vegetarian main course.

involtini di melanzane al **formaggio**

SERVES 4

Olive oil, for frying
2 large eggplants, cut lengthwise
  into slices 1/4 inch thick
2/3 cup tomato purée
1 ball of buffalo mozzarella, cut into
  slices 1/4 inch thick
Salt & freshly ground black pepper

For the stuffing
4 ounces provolone cheese, cut into
  small cubes (about 3/4 cup)
1/2 heaped cup pine nuts
1/3 cup raisins, soaked in
  water until plump, then drained
1/4 cup olive oil
2 tablespoons fresh white
  bread crumbs
1 garlic clove, minced
2 tablespoons freshly grated
  Parmesan
1 tablespoon chopped fresh basil
1 egg, beaten

Preheat the oven to 375°F. Heat a generous quantity of olive oil in a frying pan and fry the eggplant slices a few at a time until golden on both sides, adding more oil if necessary. Drain on paper towels and let cool.

For the stuffing, mix together the provolone, pine nuts, raisins, olive oil, bread crumbs, garlic, Parmesan, and basil. Season to taste and bind together with the egg. Lay out the cooked eggplant slices on a work surface and divide the stuffing among them. Roll them up fairly tightly to secure the filling and season with salt and pepper. Lightly grease a gratin dish with a little olive oil and put the eggplant rolls in it, packing them in tightly.
Pour the tomato purée and arrange the mozzarella slices down the center. Drizzle with a little more olive oil and grind some salt and pepper over. Bake in the oven for 25–30 minutes, until golden. Cool slightly before serving.

PG TIPS
Although this is usually eaten hot, I was once served it cold by an Italian friend whose mother swore that it tasted better cold the next day. You know, I think I have to agree with her. Why not try it, and judge for yourself?

Many people have rosemary bushes growing in their garden but only ever think to put this herb with lamb. Try it in this vegetarian dish and you'll find it partners the zucchini surprisingly well. I suggest you serve the clafoutis as a light main course.

zucchini & **cantal** clafoutis with rosemary

SERVES 4

2 tablespoons all-purpose flour
3 eggs
2 cups milk
12 ounces zucchini, preferably
  half yellow & half green ones, cut
  into slices 1/2 inch thick
1 garlic clove, minced
1 tablespoon chopped fresh
  rosemary, plus a few leaves
  to garnish
5 ounces Cantal, thinly sliced
Salt & freshly ground black pepper

Alternative cheese
Cheddar, mild Manchego, or
Gorwydd Caerphilly

Preheat the oven to 400°F. Beat the flour, eggs, and milk together to make a smooth batter (or whizz them in a blender). Leave to stand for 20 minutes. Cook the zucchini in boiling salted water for 30 seconds, then drain well and dry them. Arrange them in overlapping circles on the bottom of a buttered 9-inch gratin dish or flan dish and then season with salt and pepper.

Stir the garlic and chopped rosemary into the batter and pour it over the zucchini. Lay the cheese slices on top, scatter over a few rosemary leaves, and bake for 30–35 minutes, until golden and well puffed up. Serve warm rather than hot. The clafoutis will sink before serving, so don't be alarmed.

PG TIPS
This recipe makes a good blueprint for all sorts of variations. Try substituting butternut squash for the zucchini, or mushrooms that have been lightly sautéed with garlic, or even a combination of winter squash and mushrooms.

If I am truly honest this dish is only really at its best when the vegetables and cheese can be cooked over charcoal. Using a ridged cast iron grill does the job but does not compare in flavor. Not surprisingly, for me, this dish features more often during the hot summer months.

roasted vegetables with **haloumi** & salsa verde

SERVES 4

4 plum tomatoes, halved
2 medium zucchini, thickly sliced
8 baby leeks, trimmed
12 asparagus spears, peeled
4 tablespoons olive oil
14 ounces haloumi cheese
Salt & freshly ground black pepper

for the salsa verde
3 1/2 ounces fresh flat-leaf
  parsley leaves
2 anchovy fillets
1 teaspoon capers
10 large fresh mint leaves
1/2 cup olive oil

Alternative cheeses
Isle of Mull or mild Parmesan

Preheat the oven to 350°F. Arrange the vegetables in a baking pan, drizzle half the olive oil over and season. Bake in the oven for 30 minutes or until the vegetables are soft and lightly caramelized. Alternatively, grill over charcoal.

Cut the haloumi into 1/2 inch thick slices.

Heat the remaining oil in a large nonstick frying pan. When it is hot, add the haloumi slices, and cook for 1–2 minutes on each side, until golden brown.

Meanwhile, place all the ingredients for the salsa verde in a small blender and blitz to a course paste.

Arrange the roasted vegetables on 4 serving plates and top with the crisp haloumi. Spoon over the salsa verde and serve.

Every cook has a fantastic recipe for the creamy potato gratin and I'm no exception. Choosing the right waxy potatoes is very important and I always add a little Dijon mustard to the base. Here's the difference: the potatoes are topped with a crumbly cheese crust–delicious!

potato gratin with **vermont brabander** crumble

SERVES 4

2 pounds waxy potatoes (Maris Peer, Roseval, Charlotte)
2 garlic cloves, minced
10 tablespoons unsalted butter
2 eggs, beaten
1 cup heavy cream
2 cups milk
2 tablespoons Dijon mustard
8 ounces finely grated Vermont Brabander cheese (about 1 cup)
1 teaspoon fresh thyme leaves
2 cups fresh white bread crumbs
2 tablespoons olive oil
Salt & freshly ground black pepper

Alternative cheese
Lancashire

Preheat the oven to 375°F. Peel the potatoes, slice them 1/8 inch thick on a kitchen mandolin or with a knife.

Take a large ovenproof dish, rub it lightly with half the garlic, and then rub over a little butter. Arrange the potatoes in the dish in overlapping slices, seasoning liberally between each layer. Set aside.

In a bowl, whisk together the eggs, cream, milk, and mustard. Pour the mixture over the potatoes and cover them. Dot with the remaining butter.

Place the potatoes in the oven to cook for 50 minutes–1 hour or until the potatoes are tender. (If the potatoes start coloring too much, cover them with foil, by which time most of the cream will have been absorbed.)

In a bowl mix the cheese, thyme, and bread crumbs with the olive oil. Sprinkle the cheese mixture liberally over the potatoes and then return to the oven to bake until golden and crispy in texture.

Allow it to cool slightly before serving directly at your serving table for your guests to tuck in.

These meatless sausages from Wales are also known as Glamorgan sausages and are usually made with Caerphilly or Cheddar cheese and leeks. My favorite version uses Kirkham's Lancashire or sometimes Cornish Yarg. Serve the sausages with a tomato sauce or chutney.

herb cheese sausages

SERVES 4

1^1/$_2$ cups Lancashire or Cornish Yarg, grated
4^1/$_2$ cups fresh white bread crumbs, plus 2–2^1/$_2$ cups for coating
2 scallions or small leeks, minced
1 teaspoon mustard powder
1 teaspoon fresh thyme leaves
1 teaspoon chopped fresh rosemary
Freshly grated nutmeg
2 eggs, separated
Flour, for dusting
Vegetable oil, for deep- or shallow-frying
Salt & freshly ground black pepper

Alternative cheeses
Berkswell, Cheddar, Cheshire, or Gorwydd Caerphilly

Mix together the cheese, bread crumbs, scallions or leeks, mustard, and herbs. Season with nutmeg, salt, and pepper, then add the egg yolks and knead well to form a soft paste that holds its shape. Chill to firm the mixture slightly, then shape it into 12 sausages.

Whisk the egg whites just until frothy. Dust the sausages in flour, then dip them in the egg whites, and finally roll them in bread crumbs until thoroughly coated. Deep- or shallow-fry the sausages for 3–4 minutes, or until golden, turning them occasionally. Drain on paper towels and serve.

This is more of a "pudding soufflé" than a heavy pudding. Softer and quicker to ripen than Cheddar, Lancashire is the ultimate toasting cheese. Kirkham's Lancashire is the very best and, although it is usually served only on good cheeseboards, I find it hard to resist using it in cooking too.

lancashire cheese, onion & corn pudding

SERVES 4

4 tablespoons unsalted butter, plus
   extra for greasing
1 onion, minced
1 large ear of corn
1½ cups milk
⅓ cup all-purpose flour
½ teaspoon Dijon mustard
1 heaped cup grated Kirkham's
   Lancashire cheese
Freshly grated nutmeg
4 eggs, separated
Salt & freshly ground black pepper

For the sauce
½ cup Vegetable Stock (see page 16)
4 tablespoons unsalted butter,
   chilled & diced
2 tomatoes, skinned, seeded
   & chopped
½ cup fava beans, cooked
10 fresh basil leaves, shredded

Alternative cheeses
Wensleydale or Gorwydd Caerphilly

Preheat the oven to 350°F. Heat 2 tablespoons of the butter in a heavy pan, add the onion, cover, and sweat until tender. Shuck the corn, then cut off the kernels. Add them to the onion and sweat for 5 minutes, until soft. Meanwhile, cut the corncob into small pieces and place in a pan with the milk. Bring to a boil and simmer for 5 minutes to infuse the milk, then strain.

When the corn and onion are cooked, remove from the pan. Set aside 1 tablespoon of the corn kernels to use in the sauce. Add the remaining butter to the pan, sprinkle in the flour, and stir for 1–2 minutes to form a roux. Pour the infused milk on to the roux a little at a time, blending it in well and stirring constantly to make a thick sauce. Stir in the mustard, cheese, onion, and corn and season to taste with nutmeg, salt and pepper. Remove from the heat and cool slightly, then beat in the egg yolks.

Whisk the egg whites until stiff enough to hold their shape. Beat a third of the whites into the corn and cheese mixture, then gently fold in the remaining whites.

Lightly butter four 1-cup soufflé dishes and fill them two-thirds full with the mixture. Place in a roasting pan containing enough hot water to come at least halfway up the sides of the dishes. Bake for 20 minutes, until risen and lightly set.

Meanwhile, make the sauce. Bring the stock to a boil in a small pan and boil for 2 minutes. Remove from the heat and whisk in the chilled butter, a few pieces at a time, to form an emulsion. Stir in the tomatoes, fava beans, reserved corn kernels, and basil. Season to taste with salt and pepper.

When the puddings are done, cool them slightly before unmolding them out onto serving plates. Pour the sauce around and serve immediately.

PG TIPS
I find that eggs that are about 1 week old are best for soufflés. I've no idea why! Don't let the cheese and corn mixture become completely cold before adding the beaten egg whites, or the puddings will not rise to their full extent.

A simple but great-tasting vegetable dish to serve with meat, or fish, or even as a breakfast accompaniment. Try the potato cakes for brunch, topped with a poached egg and Hollandaise sauce as a variation on eggs Benedict.

potato cakes with **ricotta** & chives

SERVES 4

1¹/₂ pounds potatoes
4 tablespoons unsalted butter
2 shallots, minced
¹/₂ cup all-purpose flour
1 egg
1 egg yolk
¹/₃ cup firm ricotta cheese
2 tablespoons chopped fresh chives
Freshly grated nutmeg
3 tablespoons clarified butter
  (see Tip on page 83) or
  vegetable oil
Salt & freshly ground black pepper

Alternative cheeses
Fresh goat cheese or a grated
hard cheese

Cook the potatoes in their skins in simmering salted water until tender, then drain well. Peel and press through a potato slicer or sieve while still hot; you will need 2 cups potato purée. Heat the butter in a pan, add the shallots and sweat until tender but not colored. Stir in the flour to make a thick roux and cook for 1 minute over a low heat. Remove from the heat. Beat in the egg and egg yolk and then beat in the potato purée, ricotta, and chives. Season with nutmeg, salt and pepper and then leave to cool.

Shape the mixture into 8 potato cakes and fry in the clarified butter or oil for 4–5 minutes on each side, until golden. Serve immediately.

PG TIPS
You can use the potato cake mixture to make delicious gnocchi, by rolling it into small balls and poaching them in boiling salted water. Put them in a gratin dish, pour a richly flavored tomato sauce on top, and sprinkle them with grated Parmesan or Cheddar cheese. Then brown the gnocchi under the broiler.

This potato and cheese mash is particularly good served with roast or grilled chicken or lamb.

goat cheese & parsley mash

SERVES 4

1³/₄ pounds potatoes, peeled & cut
  into chunks
1 cup milk, warmed
4 tablespoons unsalted
  softened butter
4 ounces soft goat cheese
  such as Roubiliac, pressed through
  a sieve (about ¹/₂ cup)
2 tablespoons chopped fresh
  flat-leaf parsley
Freshly grated nutmeg
Salt & freshly ground black pepper

Put the potatoes in a pan of cold salted water and bring to a boil, then simmer until tender. Drain the potatoes and, while still hot, put them through a potato slicer or mash well.

Beat in the warm milk and the butter, then fold in the sieved goat cheese and parsley. Season with nutmeg, salt, and pepper and serve immediately.

PG TIPS
When it comes to preparing potato mash of any kind, I believe there is no better potato than the Desirée, with its superb dry texture and good flavor. It is well worth making the effort to find this variety.

Rutabaga is, sadly, rather unpopular, yet in the right hands it can be one of the most flavorful vegetables. Potato mashes are always fashionable, but perhaps rutubaga mash is the one to watch for the future! This recipe is also good when made with parsnips.

rutabaga mash with **cheddar** & black pepper butter

SERVES 4

1¹/₂ pounds rutabaga, peeled & cut
  into small cubes
2 tablespoons olive oil
¹/₄ cup milk
1 cup grated mild Cheddar cheese
5 tablespoons unsalted butter
1 teaspoon cracked black pepper
  (see Tip)
Salt

Cook the rutabaga in boiling salted water until tender, then drain well. Purée in a blender with the oil and milk until smooth. Transfer to a clean pan and heat through, then beat in the Cheddar and 1 tablespoon of the butter. Season with salt to taste, then transfer to a warmed serving dish.

Melt the remaining butter with the cracked black pepper, pour it over the purée and serve immediately.

PG TIPS
To make cracked black pepper, put some peppercorns in a small bowl and break them up roughly with the end of a rolling pin, or use a mortar and pestle.

chapter 7 **cold & warm desserts**

Sambuca is an Italian anise liqueur. If you don't have any, you could use a fruit brandy or ordinary brandy instead. This easy dessert makes a great finale to a barbecue.

sambuca-flamed **ricotta** with chilled summer berries

SERVES 4

1 cup firm ricotta cheese
¼ cup sugar, or to taste
½ cup Sambuca
½ cup heavy cream, semi-whipped
1½–2 cups mixed berries,
  such as raspberries, strawberries
  & red currants, chilled
3 ounces white chocolate, cut
  into shavings (optional)

Beat the ricotta, sugar, and 3 tablespoons of the Sambuca together until creamy. Gently fold in the heavy cream and transfer to a serving bowl. Chill for at least 4 hours.

Just before serving, heat the remaining Sambuca in a small pan until very hot and pour it over the ricotta mixture. Ignite with a match; then, when the flames have died down, top with the chilled summer berries. Finish with the white chocolate shavings, if using, and serve immediately.

PG TIPS
Try serving this with a fresh berry coulis on the side. The addition of a few toasted, slivered almonds and a little sprig of mint makes an attractive decoration and alternative to the chocolate shavings.

For an interesting contrast, you could serve the rhubarb and punch syrup with the sherbet while they are still warm.

rhubarb in chilled punch syrup with **cheese** sherbet

SERVES 4

1¹/₂ cups red wine
¹/₄ cup grenadine syrup
Juice & grated zest of 1 orange
1 cinnamon stick
¹/₂ cup sugar
1¹/₄ pounds rhubarb, peeled &
  cut into 2-inch lengths
  (about 7 cups)

For the cheese sherbet
2¹/₂ cups milk
Scant 1 cup sugar
Juice & grated zest of
  1 small orange
³/₄ cup cream cheese

For the sherbet, put the milk, sugar, orange juice and zest in a pan and bring to a boil, stirring to dissolve the sugar. Remove from the heat and let cool. Stir this mixture into the cream cheese. Pour into an ice cream machine and freeze until firm, following the manufacturer's instructions.

If you don't have an ice cream machine, pour the mixture into a shallow container and put it in the freezer. After about 30 minutes, when the mixture is beginning to set, remove from the freezer and beat well with an electric mixer or whisk to disperse any ice crystals, then return it to the freezer. Repeat this 2 or 3 times and then freeze until firm.

For the punch syrup, put the wine, grenadine syrup, orange juice and zest, cinnamon and sugar into a pan and boil until reduced to half its original volume.

Add the rhubarb to the syrup and cook gently for up to 5 minutes, until the rhubarb is tender and sweet but still holds its shape. Transfer to a bowl and let cool, then chill thoroughly. Serve with scoops of the cheese sherbet.

I first prepared this unusual dessert to an influential group of food press with great aplomb! On that occasion, apples were used instead of pears in the filling, but either are delicious. I particularly like to serve this charlotte with a large dollop of clotted cream.

pear, **jarlsberg** & date charlotte

SERVES 6

1 pound stale bread
  (approx 12–15 slices)
Softened unsalted butter

For the filling
13 ounces pears
4 tablespoons unsalted butter
1/4 cup sugar
2 tablespoons soaked raisins
3 ounces pitted dates, cut into pieces
  (about 1/2 cup)
2 tablespoons chopped walnuts
1/2 cup grated Jarlsberg cheese

For the apricot sauce
9 ounces peeled fresh apricots or
  canned in their syrup
2 tablespoons apricot brandy
Juice of 1/2 lime

To serve
Clotted cream or pouring cream
  and a little confectioners' sugar to
  dust the charlottes

Alternative cheeses
Wensleydale

Preheat the oven to 425°F. Cut 12 slices of the bread into disks, to fit the bottoms of 6 large metal dessert molds, as well as 6 to fit the tops. Cut away the crusts of the remaining slices of bread and cut into 1-inch fingers. Butter all the bread on one side only. Place a disk butter-side down in the bottom of each mold. The fingers can now easily be laid, butter-side against the mold, slightly overlapping all the way around. Place to one side.

For the filling, peel the pears, remove the center cores, and cut into 1/2-inch chunks. Melt half the butter in a pan and, when hot, add the pear and cook for 1 minute, before adding the sugar. Continue cooking for another few minutes until the pears are golden. Add the raisins, dates, and walnuts, and mix well. Remove from the heat and mix in the Jarlsberg.

Divide the mixture between the 6 lined charlottes and then top with the lids. Any excess bread at the sides can be folded over, to keep the lids in place. Bake in the oven for 20–25 minutes, until golden and crisp.

Meanwhile, prepare a quick apricot sauce by blending the apricots and their syrup to a purée in a blender. Add the apricot brandy and lime juice and mix well.

Once the charlottes are cooked, remove them from the oven and let rest for 2–3 minutes, then turn out the charlottes onto plates. Dust lightly with icing sugar. Garnish with the clotted cream and serve with the apricot sauce.

You may be surprised by this combination of caramelized apples, sweet blackberries, and savory camembert cheese. But, prepared in the style of a classic brulée, the flavors work really well together and make a sensational dessert. Be sure to serve with lashings of heavy cream.

toffee apple **camembert** & blackberry pudding

SERVES 8

2 tablespoons unsalted butter

6 tablespoons caster sugar

4 granny smith apples, peeled, cored, and diced

1/3 cup calvados apple brandy

1 cup milk

2 cups whipping cream

4 1/2 ounces Coeur De Lion Camembert cheese, cut into small dice

6 egg yolks

1 teaspoon vanilla extract

3 1/2 ounces quince jelly

8 slices brioche (or white bread)

11 ounces blackberries

Icing sugar to dust

Preheat the oven to 300°F. Heat the butter in a nonstick frying pan over a low heat, add the diced apple and half of the sugar and cook for 10–12 minutes, until the apple is caramelized. Flambé with the brandy and set aside to cool.

Put the milk and three quarters of the caramelized apple in a blender and blitz until smooth. In a pan, simmer the cream with the apple mixture, add the diced camembert, and allow to dissolve, but do not boil.

In a bowl, combine the egg yolk, remaining sugar, and vanilla extract. Mix well until light and fluffy. Pour the cream mixture into the yolks while stirring constantly, and then strain through a fine strainer.

Melt the quince jelly with 3 tablespoons of water in a pan until dissolved. Cut the brioche slices in half diagonally and then brush both sides with the quince mixture. Layer the bread, the remaining caramelized apples, and the blackberries neatly in a shallow ovenproof dish. Pour over the apple cheese cream.

Place the dish in a large baking dish. Add enough boiling water to come halfway up the sides of the dish. Place the pudding in the oven, uncovered, for about 40–45 minutes until the cream cheese has just set and the pudding is lightly brown.

Dust with a little confectioners' sugar and glaze before serving.

PG TIPS

Serve with a little pouring cream or cider apple sherbet. Figs make a lovely alternative to the blackberries in this dish.

You may be surprised to see goat cheese in an ice cream but it gives it a delicious tanginess. The ice cream makes a wonderful foil for cherries—try it with a warm cherry tart or clafoutis. I have included instructions for freezing without an ice cream machine, though I believe that for fine-textured ice creams and sherbets you do need to invest in a machine. They are quite reasonably priced now and once you have one the possibilities are endless.

goat cheese ice cream

SERVES 8

2 1/2 cups milk
1/2 cup heavy cream
4 egg yolks
1 egg
1/2 cup sugar
4 1/2 ounces mild soft goat cheese,
   such as Sainte-Maure or
   mild Ribblesdale

Bring the milk and cream to a boil. Whisk the egg yolks, whole egg, and sugar together until thick, pale, and creamy. Pour the milk and cream slowly on to the eggs, whisking all the time. Return the mixture to the pan and stir with a wooden spoon over a gentle heat until the custard has thickened enough to coat the back of the spoon. Do not let it boil or the eggs will scramble. Remove from the heat and stir in the cheese until it has melted into the custard. Pass through a fine sieve and let cool.

Pour the mixture into an ice cream machine and freeze according to the manufacturer's instructions. If you don't have an ice cream machine, pour the custard into a shallow container and place it in the freezer. After about 30 minutes, when it is beginning to set, remove it from the freezer and beat with an electric mixer or whisk to disperse any ice crystals, then return it to the freezer. Repeat 2 or 3 times and then freeze until firm.

This is a shamelessly indulgent confection, rich and sticky and quite irresistible. Make sure you buy the very best quality dates, such as the succulent Medjool variety, in order to do it justice.

brie ice cream with dates, walnuts & butterscotch sauce

SERVES 8

Ingredients for the Goat Cheese
   Ice Cream (above), replacing the
   goat cheese with 1 heaped cup
   semi-ripe Brie cheese
1 cup dates, stoned & cut into strips
2 tablespoons walnuts, in large
   pieces

For the butterscotch sauce
1/2 cup light brown sugar
1/3 cup heavy cream
6 tablespoons unsalted butter
1/2 teaspoon vanilla extract

Remove the rind from the Brie and cut the cheese into small pieces. Make the ice cream as for the Goat Cheese Ice Cream and freeze until firm.

For the sauce, put all the ingredients in a heavy saucepan and cook over a medium heat for 3–5 minutes, stirring all the time, until the color changes to a light caramel. Let cool and then chill.

To serve, put scoops of ice cream in glass coupes and scatter the dates and walnuts over. Lightly coat with the chilled butterscotch sauce.

Panna cotta, meaning "cooked cream", is a traditional Piedmontese pudding of molded cream lightly set with gelatin. Unconventionally, this recipe includes ricotta, so I have christened it Panna "Ri-cotta." Moving even further away from tradition, it is flavored with coffee and served with a fresh apricot compote.

panna "ri-cotta"

SERVES 4

1/4 cup milk
2/3 cup heavy cream
1/2 cup sugar
Grated zest of 1/2 orange
1/2 cup freshly made strong coffee,
  preferably espresso
1/2 vanilla bean, split
2 gelatin leaves
2 tablespoons rum
1 cup firm ricotta cheese,
  pressed through a sieve
Sprigs of fresh mint, to decorate
  (optional)

For the apricot compote
1/2 cup sugar
1/3 cup water
Juice of 1/2 lemon
12 ounces fresh apricots, pitted
  & sliced

Put the milk, cream, sugar, and orange zest in a pan and bring to a boil. Stir in the coffee and scrape in the seeds from the vanilla bean, then add the bean as well. Remove from the heat and let cool. Meanwhile, put the gelatin in a small pan, cover with cold water, and let soak for 5 minutes. Heat gently until the gelatin has melted.

Take the vanilla bean out of the pan and stir in the rum, sieved ricotta and the gelatin. Strain through a fine sieve, then pour into 4 ramekins or similar molds and chill for at least 2 hours, until set.

For the compote, put the sugar, water, and lemon juice in a pan and bring slowly to a boil, stirring to dissolve the sugar. Reduce the heat, add the sliced apricots, and poach for about 5 minutes, until just tender. Remove from the heat and let cool, then chill.

Unmold the coffee ricotta custards, or serve them in the ramekins if you prefer, accompanied by the apricot compote and decorated with sprigs of mint, if desired.

In this sumptuous dessert, crushed caramelized nuts are folded into a quark and whipped cream mixture which is used to fill meringue shells. The pavlovas are then decorated with candied pineapple rings. The recipe looks quite complicated, but all the separate components can be prepared well in advance and then put together shortly before serving.

crunchy **quark** pavlovas with caramelized pineapple

SERVES 6

4 egg whites
1 cup plus 2 tablespoons
  superfine sugar
1 teaspoon vinegar
1 cup quark
1 cup heavy cream

For the Florentine
6 tablespoons sugar
2/3 cup chopped hazelnuts
3/4 cup slivered almonds

For the carmelized pineapple
1/2 cup sugar
1 cup water
1 small, ripe pineapple, peeled,
  cored & thinly sliced into rings

The pavlovas can be prepared a day in advance. Preheat the oven to 225°F. Whisk the egg whites until they form stiff peaks and then gradually whisk in two-thirds of the superfine sugar and the vinegar. Fold in the rest of the superfine sugar by hand. Take 6 metal rings, each 3 inches in diameter, place them on a baking sheet and fill with the meringue (alternatively pipe it into disks on parchment paper). Carefully remove the disks. Bake the meringues for 1–1½ hours, until crisp on the outside. Let cool in the turned-off oven.

For the Florentine, put the sugar in a heavy-based pan and melt over a medium heat, then raise the heat and cook until the sugar syrup is a deep golden brown. Stir in the nuts with a wooden spoon. Pour the mixture on to a lightly oiled baking sheet, spreading it evenly, and let cool until hard. Place the nut caramel in a small plastic bag and crush to large crumbs with the end of a rolling pin–or use a food processor.

For the caramelized pineapple, bring the sugar and water to a boil. Add the pineapple rings, reduce the heat, and cook gently for about 30–45 minutes, until the pineapple becomes translucent. Let cool in the syrup.

Whisk the quark and cream together until thick, then fold in the crushed Florentine, reserving about 2 tablespoons to decorate the pavlovas.

To serve, turn the meringues over and carefully scoop out the center from the bottom of each one, leaving a thin shell. Fill them with the quark cream and turn right-side up again. Place on individual serving plates and decorate with the slices of pineapple. Drizzle the pineapple syrup over and sprinkle with the reserved Florentine.

This looks like a classic crème brûlée, but when you shatter the crisp caramel topping a thin layer of dark chocolate is revealed underneath. You could put a handful of raspberries at the bottom of each dish for another unexpected treat.

chocolate **mascarpone** brûlée

SERVES 4

2 cups mascarpone
1 cup granulated sugar
6 egg yolks
2 ounces bittersweet chocolate
Confectioners' sugar, for dusting

Preheat the oven to 275°F. Lightly whisk together the cheese, two-thirds of the granulated sugar, and all the egg yolks and then strain through a sieve. Pour the mixture into 4 ramekins and place them on a wad of newspaper in a roasting pan (the paper prevents the mixture at the bottom of the dishes getting too hot). Pour boiling water into the roasting pan to come halfway up the sides of each dish and bake for 30–35 minutes, or until the custards are just firm to the touch. Remove from the oven, take the dishes out of the roasting pan and let cool, then chill thoroughly.

Melt the chocolate and spread it evenly over each mascarpone custard. Return them to the refrigerator to chill for 15 minutes so the chocolate sets hard, then sprinkle the remaining granulated sugar over the top. Place under the broiler, close to the heat sources until the sugar is golden and bubbling, then let cool. Dust the edges with a little confectioners' sugar before serving.

PG TIPS
A very effective method is to use a small domestic blowtorch to glaze the brûlées instead of putting them under the broiler.

Purple figs are best for this dish. During summer I like to serve some fresh berries sprinkled around the figs.

poached figs stuffed with **sainte-maure** cheese in merlot wine syrup

SERVES 4

16 ripe but firm figs
4 ounces Sainte-Maure goat cheese
1/4 cup mascarpone cheese
Grated zest of 1 lemon
2 tablespoons sugar

For the syrup
1/2 cup sugar
1 bottle of Merlot (or other red wine)
1 cinnamon stick

Alternative cheeses
Any soft goat cheese such as mild Ribblesdale or Montrachet. The Australian Kervella goat ricotta makes an interesting alternative

For the syrup, put the sugar, wine, and cinnamon in a saucepan that is just large enough to hold the figs in a single layer. Bring slowly to a boil, stirring to dissolve the sugar, and simmer for 4–5 minutes. Add the figs and poach for 4–5 minutes, or until just tender. Remove the figs with a slotted spoon. Boil the syrup until reduced to half its original volume.

Purée 4 of the figs in a blender, adding enough of the reduced poaching syrup to give a saucelike consistency. Strain and chill.

Beat together the Sainte-Maure, mascarpone, lemon zest, and sugar. Slice the tops off the 12 remaining figs, fill with the cheese mixture, and replace the tops. Arrange the figs on 4 serving plates, pour the sauce around, and serve.

The caramel offsets the sharpness of the yogurt cheese, resulting in a simple dessert with complex flavors. This is really quite a straightforward recipe, but you need to start preparations 3–4 days in advance, in order to drain the yogurt for the labna.

pepper-caramel roasted pears with **labna**

SERVES 4

1 cup live strained plain yogurt
1/2 teaspoon ground cinnamon
2/3 cup packed brown sugar
3/4 cup water
1 cinnamon stick, broken into
  3 pieces
1/4 teaspoon cracked black pepper
  (see Tip on page 146)
4 ripe but firm Bartlett pears
4 tablespoons unsalted butter
1/3 cup Poire William or brandy

Alternative cheeses
**A blue cheese like Dolcelatte Torta
or curd cheese also goes well with
the pears**

Mix the plain yogurt with the ground cinnamon and then drain it in cheesecloth for 3–4 days, as described in the recipe for Labna on page 185.

Preheat the oven to 350°F. Put the sugar in a heavy-based saucepan and leave over a low heat until melted. Raise the heat until it has caramelized lightly, then carefully pour in the water (the syrup may splutter). Add the cinnamon stick and cracked black pepper. Boil for 10–12 minutes to form a light syrup.

Peel the pears carefully so as to keep their shape, then cut them in half, leaving the stems intact. Remove the cores.

Heat the butter in a large, shallow casserole or an ovenproof frying pan, add the pear halves, flat-side down, and cook until lightly colored. Pour over the Poire William or brandy, turn the pears over, then pour the syrup over. Transfer to the oven and bake for 40 minutes, basting the pears with the syrup once or twice to form a light glaze. Remove from the oven and let cool to room temperature. To serve, top each pear half with a scoop of the labna.

Try to get really good prunes for this, preferably French Agen prunes or the large, moist Californian prunes. I like to serve the tart with a fresh orange sauce, such as the one with My Favorite Pick-Me-Up on page 152.

quark, prune & white chocolate tart

SERVES 4–6

¹/₂ quantity of sweet pastry
  (see page 21)
4 ounces white chocolate
2 gelatin leaves
¹/₄ cup dry white wine
Juice & grated zest of 1 orange
4 egg yolks
2 tablespoons sugar
¹/₂ heaped cup quark
²/₃ cup heavy cream, semi-whipped
10 prunes, soaked overnight in
¹/₄ cup Armagnac or brandy

Alternative cheese
Any curd cheese

Preheat the oven to 375°F. Roll out the pastry and use to line an 8-inch tart pan. Line with parchment paper, fill with ceramic baking beans and bake for 8–10 minutes. Remove the paper and beans and bake for a further 5 minutes. Take out of the oven and let cool.

Melt the white chocolate in a small bowl set over a pan of hot water. Brush the base of the cooled pastry case with about two-thirds of the melted chocolate and set aside.

Cover the gelatine leaves with a little water and leave to soak for 5 minutes. Bring the wine, orange juice, and zest to a boil in a pan. Whisk together the egg yolks and sugar in a bowl for 2–3 minutes, until creamy. Gradually pour the wine and orange mixture on to the yolks, whisking all the time. Cool slightly, then add the soaked and drained gelatin leaves and stir until completely melted. Fold in the remaining melted chocolate.

When the mixture is almost cold and just beginning to set, gently but thoroughly fold in the quark and the semi-whipped cream. Arrange the prunes in the pastry case, then pour in the filling. Chill for at least 2 hours for it to set.

PG TIPS
Don't serve the tart too cold, as this impairs the flavor. Remove it from the refrigerator and bring it to room temperature about 15 minutes before serving.

I devised this recipe for the Christmas edition of the BBC Vegetarian Good Food magazine, when looking for an alternative to the traditional Christmas plum pudding.

dried fruit & **mascarpone** fool with saffron & ginger syrup

SERVES 6–8

1 pound dried apricots
2 1/2 cups water
1 cup mixed dried fruit, such as apricots, prunes & figs, cut into large pieces
1/2 cup sugar
Juice & zest of 1 lemon
6 tablespoons apricot brandy (or orange liqueur such as cointreau or Grand Marnier)
1 1/4 cups heavy cream
1/2 cup mascarpone cheese
Sprigs of fresh mint, to decorate (optional)

For the saffron & ginger syrup
2 tablespoons syrup from a jar of stem ginger
Juice & grated zest of 1 orange
1 cup water
A good pinch of saffron strands

Put the dried apricots in a saucepan, pour the water over and let soak overnight. Bring all the ingredients for the saffron and ginger syrup to a boil, pour it over the mixed dried fruit, and let that soak overnight too.

The next day, bring the dried apricots to a boil, then reduce the heat and simmer for 20–25 minutes until soft, adding a little more water if necessary. Transfer to a blender and add the sugar, lemon juice, and zest and apricot brandy. Blitz to a smooth purée. Let cool.

Whip the cream until it is just beginning to thicken. Beat the mascarpone just to soften it and then fold it gently into the cream. Fold two-thirds of the apricot purée into this mixture. Pour the fool into tall glasses to half-fill them. Put a spoonful of the remaining apricot purée on top and then add more fool, until the mixture is 3/4 inch below the rim of the glasses. Chill for 4 hours.

To serve, top up the glasses with the mixed dried fruit in syrup and decorate with the mint sprigs, if using.

No book on cheese cookery would be complete without a recipe for cheesecake. I prefer the uncooked variety, so here is one of my favorites that I make at home, using autumn produce. If you can't get wild loganberries, try blackberries, blueberries, or raspberries, or a mixture.

wild loganberry & roasted hazelnut **cheesecake**

2 eggs, separated
$1/2$ cup sugar
8 ounces wild loganberries (about $11/2$ cups), plus a few extra to decorate
2 gelatin leaves
$11/2$ cups full-fat cream cheese
$2/3$ heavy cream, semi-whipped

For the base
1 packed cup graham-cracker crumbs
2 tablespoons raw brown or light brown sugar
3 tablespoons roasted & chopped hazelnuts (see Tip on page 73)
4 tablespoons melted unsalted butter

For the sauce
8 ounces wild loganberries
Juice of 1 lemon, or to taste
Sugar, to taste

For the base, put the graham-cracker crumbs in a bowl and stir in the brown sugar, chopped hazelnuts, and melted butter. The mixture should be sticky but not wet. Press it firmly over the bottom of an 8-inch springform cake pan.

Put the egg yolks and sugar in a bowl set over a pan of simmering water, making sure the water is not touching the base of the bowl. Whisk with a portable electric maker until the mixture is thick and creamy in color; the beaters should leave a trail on the surface when lifted. Remove the bowl from the pan of water and let cool, whisking occasionally.

Purée the loganberries in a blender and then push through a fine sieve. Put the gelatin in a pan with 3 tablespoons water and leave for 5 minutes, then place over a very low heat until melted and clear. Mix the puréed loganberries with the egg yolk mixture, then stir in the melted gelatin. Add the cream cheese and mix in thoroughly. Whisk the egg whites until stiff and fold them in. Finally, fold in the whipped cream. Pour the mixture into the cake pan and smooth the top with a metal spatula. Chill for at least 2 hours, until set.

Meanwhile, make the sauce. Put the loganberries in a blender with the lemon juice and a little sugar and blitz until smooth. Pass through a fine sieve and add a little more lemon juice or sugar to taste, if necessary. Serve the cheesecake with the sauce, decorated with a few extra loganberries, if desired.

Here, the famous crémet d'Anjou mixture of cream and soft cheese is blended with a tart blackberry purée and used as a filling between caramelized pastry wafers. It is quite some combination.

caramelized pastry wafers with blackberry **crémet**

SERVES 4

1 cup cream cheese or
  fromage blanc
1 cup heavy cream or crème
  fraîche, semi-whipped
2 egg whites
2 tablespoons granulated sugar
4 ounces puff pastry
3/4 confectioners' sugar

For the blackberry purée
8 ounces fresh blackberries
  (about 1 1/2 cups)
1/2 cup sugar
A little lemon juice

Put the cream cheese or fromage blanc in a bowl and beat until smooth, then fold in the whipped cream or crème fraîche. Whisk the egg whites until they form stiff peaks. Fold in the sugar. Fold the egg whites into the cream cheese mixture. Set aside.

Put half of the blackberries in a blender, add the sugar and blitz to a purée. Transfer to a bowl and balance the sweetness with a squeeze of lemon juice. Add half the purée to the cheese mixture and gently fold it through to give a marbled effect. Cover and refrigerate for about 12 hours, preferably overnight.

Preheat the oven to 425°F. For the pastry wafers, roll out the puff pastry in a rectangle about 6 by 10 inches and approximately 1/6 inch thick. Dust with a little of the confectioners' sugar, then roll it up very tightly like a jelly roll. Place in a very cold refrigerator or a freezer for a short while to firm up, then with a sharp knife cut the roll into 12 slices about 1/4 inch thick. (You won't need all the pastry but you can freeze the rest for later use.) Liberally dust the slices with the remaining confectioners' sugar and roll them out as thinly as possible into ovals. Place them on a baking sheet and bake for 8–10 minutes, or until golden and caramelized. Remove from the oven and place on a wire rack to cool.

To serve, put a wafer on each of 4 serving plates and cover with some of the marbled cheese mixture. Place another wafer on top, cover with more cheese mixture, then top with a final wafer. Stir the remaining blackberries into the remaining purée and arrange around the wafer stacks.

PG TIPS
Pipe the cheese mixture over the pastry wafers for a professional finish. These crisp pastry wafers are also good as an accompaniment to ice cream or sherbet. They keep for up to a week in a sealed container in a dry, cool place.

I love the refreshing taste of these summer berries, offset with a sweet cheese sauce. Other fruit such as apricots or peaches can be used, or even poached pears during the colder months. Why not try serving the apricot Stilton sauce as a fondue for dipping fruits? In this case, a little apricot brandy could be added instead of kirsch.

summer fruit gratin with apricot **stilton** sauce

SERVES 4

8 ounces fresh blackberries
  (about 1½ cups)
¼ cup sugar, or to taste
1 pound mixed fresh
  summer berries, such as
  strawberries, blackberries,
  raspberries, red currants
  (about 3 cups)

For the sauce
⅓ cup heavy cream
¾ cup grated white apricot
  Stilton cheese
2 egg yolks
¼ cup sugar
Kirsch, to taste

Alternative cheeses
Any cream cheese could be
substituted for the Stilton

Place the blackberries in a blender with the sugar and blitz to a purée. Strain the purée through a fine sieve to remove the seeds. Taste and add more sugar if desired.

For the sauce, bring the cream to a boil in a pan, then remove from the heat and stir in the cheese. Let cool. Put the egg yolks and sugar in a bowl set over a pan of simmering water, making sure the water does not touch the base of the bowl. Whisk until the mixture becomes pale and thick and doubles in volume. Remove the bowl from the heat and continue to whisk until the mixture is cold. Fold in the cheese and cream mixture and then add kirsch to taste.

Toss the mixed berries with the blackberry purée and pile them up in the center of 4 heatproof serving plates. Carefully pour the cheese sauce around the fruit and put the plates under the broiler to glaze the cheese sauce until light golden in color. Serve immediately.

A simple, light, lemon-scented pancake topped with ricotta and fresh raspberries and served with raspberry sauce. I like it for dessert with a scoop of vanilla ice cream, but it also makes an excellent brunch dish. For a winter version you could fill the blini with poached pears instead of raspberries. To make chocolate blini, replace 2 tablespoons of the flour with cocoa powder.

lemon blini with **ricotta** & raspberries

SERVES 4

1^1/$_2$ tablespoons granulated sugar
Finely grated zest of 1 lemon
^{3}/$_4$ cup self-rising flour
^{1}/$_2$ teaspoon baking powder
2 teaspoons melted butter
^{2}/$_3$ cup milk
2 eggs, separated
A pinch each of salt & sugar
1 tablespoon olive oil
^{1}/$_4$ cup ricotta cheese, drained
8 ounces fresh raspberries
  (about 2 cups)
Confectioners' sugar, for dusting
Sprigs of fresh mint, to decorate
  (optional)

For the sauce
8 ounces fresh raspberries
Juice of ^{1}/$_2$ lemon, or to taste
^{3}/$_4$ cup confectioners' sugar,
  or to taste

Alternative cheese
Quark, Marscapone or
Brillat Savarin

For the blini, mix together the sugar and lemon zest to extract the lemon's natural oils. Sift the flour and baking powder into a bowl and stir in the sugar mixture. In a separate bowl, whisk together the melted butter, milk and egg yolks, then combine with the flour to make a batter. Whisk the egg whites with a pinch of salt and sugar until they form stiff peaks, then fold them into the batter. Let stand for 5–10 minutes.

Meanwhile, make the sauce. Purée the raspberries in a blender, then press them through a fine sieve. Stir in the lemon juice and confectioners' sugar, adjusting the quantities to taste if necessary.

To cook the blini, heat the olive oil in a heavy-based frying pan over a gentle heat (or individual blini pans if you happen to have them). Then drop in 2 tablespoons of batter for each pancake so that they are about 4 inches in diameter. Cook for about 2 minutes, until bubbles start to appear on the surface, then flip them over and cook the other side. Keep them warm while you cook the remaining blini–you need 8 in all.

Carefully spread the ricotta over 4 of the blini, then cover with the raspberries. Top with the other 4 blini and put on serving plates. Dust with confectioners' sugar, pour the raspberry sauce around and serve, decorated with sprigs of mint, if desired.

PG TIPS
I've found that boxed pancake and waffle mixes make a good alternative to the flour and baking powder, producing soft, light pancakes.

Corsican food is typically Mediterranean but has a few distinctive hallmarks, one of which is the use of Broccio, a sheep's milk cheese. Broccio is popular in savory dishes and desserts such as fritters, custards and this simple omelet. It's quite hard to obtain elsewhere, so I have substituted goat cheese, which I actually prefer.

corsican-style **goat cheese** & honey omelet

SERVES 4

6 eggs, beaten
1 tablespoon chopped fresh mint
1/3 cup granulated sugar
2/3 cup ground almonds

4 tablespoons unsalted butter
3 ounces soft goat cheese,
  such as Roubiliac, thinly sliced
2 tablespoons honey
Confectioners' sugar, for dusting

Put the eggs in a bowl with the mint, sugar, ground almonds, and 1 tablespoon cold water and beat until light and fluffy. Heat the butter in a 8-inch omelet pan. When it is foaming, pour in the beaten eggs and stir with a fork. When half set, arrange the goat cheese slices over the top. Let soften slightly, then spoon the honey over and fold the omelet–or leave it flat, if you prefer. Dust with confectioners' sugar and serve warm.

Wensleydale cheese should be eaten young and fresh and is delicious with crisp autumn fruits such as apples and pears. This pie is one of my favorite old English desserts, a traditional Yorkshire way of combining apples and cheese. In this recipe the cheese is mixed with the apples for the filling, but often it is included in the pastry instead. Another Yorkshire custom is to serve a wedge of Wensleydale with a slice of rich fruit cake or a mincemeat tartlet.

spiced apple & **wensleydale** pie

SERVES 4

1 pound apples, peeled,
  cored & chopped
A pinch of ground cloves
1 teaspoon ground cinnamon
A pinch of freshly grated nutmeg
1/3 cup raisins
1/2 cup sugar
1/2 cup Wensleydale cheese,
  broken into small chunks
1/2 quantity of basic pie pastry
  (see page 21)
1 egg beaten with 1 tablespoon
  water, to glaze

Preheat the oven to 400°F. Mix together the apples, spices, raisins, sugar, and cheese and place in an 8-inch deep pie pan. Roll out the pastry a little larger than the pie dish. Cut a thin strip from around the edge and press it on to the rim of the pan, then brush with a little of the beaten egg. Cover the pie with the pastry, pressing it on to the rim and trimming the edges. Flute the edges neatly and make a hole in the center.

Roll out the pastry trimmings and cut out leaves or whatever shape you like. Use to decorate the pie. Brush all over with the beaten egg and bake for 15–20 minutes, until the pastry is golden. Reduce the oven temperature to 325°F and bake for a further 25 minutes. Serve hot or warm, with a light custard sauce or thick whipped cream.

When we were creating recipes for this book, my sous-chefs and I came across many remarkable combinations that pleasantly surprised us. None more so than this recipe pairing prune soufflé with goat cheese ice cream, which has turned out to be one of my favorites. Try it, and I think you'll see why.

hot prune soufflé with **goat cheese** ice cream

SERVES 4

$1/2$ cup pitted prunes,
  preferably Agen prunes
3 tablespoons unsalted butter,
  plus extra for greasing
$31/2$ tablespoons all-purpose flour
1 cup milk, boiled & strained
5 eggs, separated
2 tablespoons Armagnac
$1/2$ cup superfine sugar,
  plus extra for dusting
2 tablespoons cornstarch
4 scoops of Goat Cheese Ice Cream
  (see page 154)

Lightly butter 4 soufflé dishes, each 1 cup in capacity, and then dust with a little sugar, shaking out any excess. Preheat the oven to 400°F.

Simmer the prunes in water to cover until soft. Purée them in a blender and set aside. Melt the butter in a saucepan, stir in the flour, and cook for 1–2 minutes. Gradually stir in the milk to form a thick sauce and simmer for 5 minutes. Stir in the prune purée, remove from the heat, and let cool. Beat in the egg yolks and Armagnac.

Whisk the egg whites until they form stiff peaks, then gradually whisk in the sugar. Finally, whisk in the cornstarch. Beat a third of the egg whites into the prune sauce and then gently fold in the rest. Pour the mixture into the soufflé dishes and put them in a roasting pan containing enough water to come two-thirds of the way up the sides of the dishes. Bake in the oven for 15–20 minutes, until well risen. Serve immediately, with the ice cream on the side.

PG TIPS
A nice touch is to break open the soufflés at the table and put a scoop of the Goat Cheese Ice Cream in the center of each one. You could also make extra prune purée and drizzle it over the ice cream.

Another variation on the cheese and apple pie theme (see Spiced Apple and Wensleydale Pie on page 172), this time with an Italian flavor. A simple dollop of whipping cream is all you need to accompany it, but if you prefer something a little more elaborate, try a compote of plums or prunes. Strudel pastry can be time-consuming to make, but phyllo is generally accepted as a convenient substitute nowadays.

apple **pecorino** strudel

SERVES 6–8

1 cup fresh white bread crumbs
1/2 cup ground almonds
1/2 cup unsalted butter
2 pounds apples, peeled, cored
  & thinly sliced (about 8 cups)
1/4 cup granulated sugar
1 teaspoon ground cinnamon
1/2 teaspoon apple pie spice
1/3 cup raisins, soaked in water
  until plump
1/3 cup chopped walnuts or almonds
Grated zest of 1/2 lemon
5 ounces pecorino Romano cheese,
  thinly sliced
4 large sheets of phyllo pastry, about
  18 by 12 inches
Confectioners' sugar, for dusting

Alternative cheese
Ricotta makes a tasty alternative
to the pecorino or similar firmer
cheeses like Jarlsberg

Preheat the oven to 400°F. Fry the bread crumbs and ground almonds in 4 tablespoons of the butter until lightly golden, then set aside.

Mix together the apples, granulated sugar, cinnamon, apple pie spice, raisins, nuts, and lemon zest. Carefully fold in the pecorino cheese.

Melt the remaining butter. Lay out 1 sheet of phyllo on a work surface and brush with some of the butter, then top with the remaining sheets of phyllo, brushing with butter between the layers. Brush the final sheet of pastry with more butter and sprinkle the fried bread crumb mixture over the top. Spread the apple mixture over the surface, then roll up the pastry to form a compact roll. Transfer to a greased baking sheet, curving the strudel to fit if necessary, and brush with the remaining melted butter. Bake for 20–25 minutes, until crisp and golden.

Remove from the oven, dust generously with confectioners' sugar and serve hot.

PG TIPS
If your phyllo pastry is smaller than the size given in the recipe, use extra sheets and lay them out on the work surface, overlapping the edges, to form a rectangle about 8 by 12 inches. Cover with a few more sheets to make 4 layers, brushing with melted butter as above.

These beignets are one of those sticky, Middle Eastern-style desserts with lots of honey and nuts. Rather than the usual heavy pastries, however, they are light and fluffy little fritters.

cream cheese beignets with walnut honey

SERVES 4–6

1 pound cream cheese
2 tablespoons granulated sugar
Grated zest of 1/2 lemon
1 cup all-purpose flour, sifted
2 eggs
Vegetable oil, for deep-frying
2/3 cup honey
3/4 cup chopped walnuts
Confectioners' sugar, for dusting

Put the cheese, granulated sugar, and lemon zest in a bowl and beat together until smooth. Stir in the flour a little at a time, until thoroughly combined. Beat in the eggs one at a time, then let stand for up to 1 hour.

Put the vegetable oil in a deep fryer or large saucepan and heat to 375°F. Drop heaped teaspoonfuls of the cheese mixture into the hot oil a few at a time, and fry for about 2 minutes, until golden and puffed up. Drain on paper towels and keep warm while you cook the rest.

Heat the honey and walnuts in a pan until just warm. Dust the cheese beignets with confectioners' sugar and serve with the walnut honey alongside.

Pecan pie is, deservedly, a universal favorite. The addition of blue cheese makes an interesting variation. I like to serve the pie warm with whipped cream.

cashel blue & pecan pie

SERVES 4

1/2 quantity of sweet pastry (see p21)
Flour, for dusting
5 tablespoons unsalted butter
3/4 cup golden syrup
4 ounces Cashel Blue or similar mild
  blue cheese, cut into small cubes
  (about 1 cup)
3/4 cup packed light brown sugar
3 eggs
2 tablespoons rum
1/2 teaspoon vanilla extract
A pinch of salt
1 heaped cup pecan halves

Alternative cheese
If you prefer a stronger cheese, you could use Roquefort or Gorgonzola

Preheat the oven to 375°F. Roll out the pastry on a lightly floured surface until it is 1/8 inch thick and use to line a 9-inch tart pan that is 1-inch deep. Prick the bottom with a fork, line with parchment paper and fill with ceramic baking beans. Bake for 10 minutes, then remove the paper and beans and bake for a further 5 minutes. Remove from the oven and reduce the temperature to 350°F.

Heat the butter and syrup in a pan, add half the cheese, and stir until melted. In a bowl, whisk together the sugar, eggs, rum, vanilla, and salt. Add the pecans and then stir into the syrup and cheese mixture. Add the remaining cheese and pour the mixture into the pastry shell. Bake for about 30 minutes, until just set.

Made with Neufchâtel cheese, this delicate, sweet version of croque monsieur is not unlike pain perdu, or French toast. Although it can be served for dessert, it also makes a good brunch dish or summer breakfast. Neufchâtel is a creamy, fresh-tasting cheese from Normandy, best eaten young.

croque mademoiselle

SERVES 4

1/2 cup Neufchâtel cheese
1 tablespoon Grand Marnier
Grated zest of 1/2 orange
3 tablespoons granulated sugar
8 slices of brioche (see page 22),
  crusts removed
8 ounces raspberries (about 2 cups)
2 eggs, beaten
2/3 cup heavy cream
2/3 cup milk
1 teaspoon ground cinnamon
4 tablespoons unsalted butter
Confectioners' sugar, for dusting

Alternative cheeses
If Neufchâtel is too strong for you,
replace it with quark or firm ricotta

Mix together the Neufchâtel, Grand Marnier, orange zest and 1 tablespoon of the sugar. Spread this mixture evenly over the slices of brioche. Top 4 slices with the raspberries, packing them tightly into the cheese, then put the remaining slices of brioche on top.

Beat together the eggs, cream, milk, cinnamon, and remaining sugar and pour into a shallow dish. Dip the sandwiches into this mixture on both sides. Heat the butter in a large frying pan and cook the sandwiches for about 2 minutes on each side, until golden. Remove and drain on paper towels, then dust liberally with confectioners' sugar. Serve the Croques Mademoiselles immediately, with some lightly whipped cream.

PG TIPS
You could substitute white bread for the brioche, although the flavor won't be quite as good. Some supermarkets stock light toast breads, which would work better than plain white bread.

This tart is a specialty of the Poitou region in France, where it is made with goat cheese, as below. Use cream cheese instead, if desired.

tourte de **poitou**

SERVES 6

1/2 quantity of sweet pastry (see p 21)
Flour, for dusting
6 ounces soft, unsalted goat cheese,
  such as Sainte-Maure
3 eggs
1/2 cup sugar
2 tablespoons heavy cream
3 tablespoons minced candied fruit
Grated zest of 1 orange
1 tablespoon pistachio nuts, skinned
  and chopped (use tip)

Preheat the oven to 375°F. Roll out the pastry on a lightly floured surface until it is 1/8 inch thick and use to line a 8-inch tart pan. Prick the bottom with a fork, line with parchment paper, and fill with ceramic baking beans. Bake for 10 minutes, then remove the paper and beans and return to the oven to bake for 5 minutes longer.

Meanwhile, chop the skinned pistachio nuts. Beat together all the remaining ingredients in a bowl until thoroughly combined. Pour into the pastry shell and return to the oven to bake for 45 minutes, until the top is a deep golden brown. Serve warm or, if you prefer, cold.

PG TIPS
To skin pistachio nuts, put them on a baking sheet in a fairly hot oven for 1–2 minutes, then place them in a clean dishtowel and rub gently to loosen the skins. Let cool, then peel off the skins.

Fillings for baked peaches are legion, but this combination of soft, fresh cheese, bitter chocolate, and almond cookies is especially good. Apricots can be prepared in the same way.

baked amaretti peaches with **ricotta** & bitter chocolate

SERVES 4

1¼ cups dry white wine

¼ cup Amaretto liqueur
  (optional)

½ cup sugar

½ teaspoon vanilla extract or
  1 vanilla bean, split open

4 large, ripe peaches

¼ cup firm ricotta cheese

1 cup amaretti cookies,
  crushed into small pieces

2 tablespoons grated bittersweet
  chocolate (use plain chocolate with
  at least 70% cocoa solids)

2 tablespoons semi-whipped
  heavy cream

Preheat the oven to 425°F. Bring the wine, Amaretto liqueur, if using, sugar and vanilla to a boil in a pan. Boil for 5 minutes to form a light syrup. Add the peaches and poach for 1 minute. Remove the peaches with a slotted spoon and drain well, then slip off their skins. Cut the peaches in half, following the indentation that runs around their circumference. Twist each peach to loosen both halves and then remove the pit. Using a teaspoon, carefully scoop out a little of the flesh to enlarge the cavity.

In a bowl, mix together the ricotta, crushed amaretti and chocolate, then fold in the cream. Fill the peach halves with this mixture and place them in a baking dish that is just large enough to hold them in a single layer. Pour a little of the poaching syrup into the dish around the peaches and bake for 5–8 minutes, until golden. Serve immediately, with a good vanilla ice cream.

PG TIPS

Freeze any leftover poaching syrup to make a delicately flavored peach sherbet. An ideal way to enjoy this dessert all year round is to buy your peaches in the summer and bottle them in syrup for storing. They are also delicious served in their syrup with vanilla ice cream.

This marriage of sweet and salty flavors is common in Mediterranean countries. I like to serve some crème fraîche with the turnovers, which makes for a nice contrast of temperatures.

cretan **sheep milk** turnovers with melted honey

SERVES 4

1 cup Greek feta cheese
1/4 cup cream cheese
1 egg, beaten
4 tablespoons unsalted butter,
  softened
1/4 teaspoon ground cinnamon
Juice of 1/4 lemon
2 tablespoons chopped fresh mint
Vegetable oil, for deep-frying
Confectioners' sugar, for dusting
2/3 cup honey, warmed
2/3 cup crème fraîche (optional)

For the pastry
1 2/3 cups all-purpose flour,
  plus extra for dusting
2 tablespoons sugar
2 tablespoons unsalted butter at
  room temperature, diced
About 2/3 cup water

To make the pastry, sift the flour into a bowl and stir in the sugar, then rub in the butter pieces with your fingertips to give a coarse, sandy texture. Stir in enough water to make a soft, pliable dough. Turn out on to a lightly floured work surface and knead for 4–5 minutes, until smooth and elastic.

Place the feta in a bowl and crush it to a coarse pulp with a fork. Add the cream cheese and egg and beat together until smooth. Next, beat in the butter and cinnamon, then the lemon juice and chopped mint. Set aside in the refrigerator until required.

Roll out the pastry as thinly as possible on a lightly floured surface. Cut out 16–20 rounds with a 3-inch pastry cutter. Put about 1 tablespoon of the feta filling on one half of each pastry round, brush the edges with water, then fold over and seal well to make turnovers. Place them in the refrigerator for 30 minutes to firm up.

Meanwhile, pour the vegetable oil into a deep fryer or a deep saucepan and heat to 350–375°F. Carefully slip the turnovers into the hot oil, a few at a time, and fry for about 2 minutes or until golden, turning them occasionally. Take out and drain on paper towels to remove excess oil. Keep warm while you fry the remaining turnovers.

Place the turnovers on a serving dish, sift a little confectioners' sugar over and drizzle with warm melted honey. Serve immediately, with crème fraîche, if desired.

PG TIPS
Try to find a good Greek honey to use in this recipe. If time is of the essence, you could try using phyllo pastry instead. The result will be almost as good, although the turnovers will be a little crispy.

chapter 8 alternative cheeseboard

This sweet yet savory preparation makes a great addition to a cheese board as well as a delicious alternative to a dessert. Dried cranberries and other varieties of dried fruits can easily replace the cherries.

baked **camembert** with dried cherries & caramel pecans

SERVES 4

1/2 cup kirsch liquor
3 ounces dried cherries (1/2 cup)
A whole small Camembert in
  its wooden box
1/2 cup sugar
1/2 cup water
2 ounces pecan nuts, coarsely
  broken into pieces (1/3 cup)

Heat the kirsch in a small pan with the cherries until it boils. Remove from the heat, transfer to a bowl, and let cool overnight in the refrigerator. Remove the cherries and dry of any excess liquid.

Take the camembert from its box, remove the paper wrapping and, using a small knife, insert a dozen or so tiny slits into the cheese liberally over the surface. Press the cherries into the slits.

Preheat the oven to 400°F. Arrange the camembert on a wire rack over a foil-lined baking sheet.

Place the sugar and water in a heavy pan and warm over a low heat to melt the sugar. Increase the heat and let it boil until the sugar takes on a light golden caramel color. Add the pecan pieces to create a nut caramel. Spoon over the camembert.

Place the cheese in the oven for 10–12 minutes, until the cheese is heated through and begins to soften. Cool to room temperature before serving. Cut into wedges.

A quick and simple method of marinating cheese, with basil, olive oil, and garlic. I like to serve it as part of a cheeseboard, although it also makes a good light appetizer accompanied by a small crisp salad and some bread.

simple marinated **chèvre** in basil oil

SERVES 4

4 crottin de Chavignol or aged
  Chabis goat cheeses, cut
  horizontally in half
1 bay leaf
6 black peppercorns, lightly crushed
2 garlic cloves, minced
1 handful of fresh basil leaves
1/2 cup extra-virgin olive oil, warmed
Salt

Alternative cheeses
**A creamy Camembert or Brie,
cut into slices 1/2 inch thick,
or Roubiliac goat cheese balls**

Place the cheese halves in a dish just large enough to hold them in one layer and put the bay leaf and peppercorns on top. Blitz the garlic, basil, and olive oil together in a blender to form a fairly liquid sauce and then season with salt. Pour the basil oil over the cheese, cover, and leave in a cool place for about 6 hours. It will keep for about a week in the refrigerator, but bring to room temperature before serving.

Serve this delicious cheese preserve with a good walnut bread.

pressed cheese with dried fruits

SERVES 4

4 crottin de Chavignol or aged
  Chabis goat cheeses, cut
  horizontally in half
1/3 cup dried figs, cut into quarters
1/4 cup prunes, cut in half
3 sprigs of fresh thyme
3 bay leaves
6 black peppercorns
6 tablespoons prune eau de vie
  or cognac
Olive oil

Place 2 of the cheese halves in a sterilized 2-cup preserving jar and scatter a third each of the figs and prunes over, plus a sprig of thyme, a bay leaf, and 2 peppercorns. Sprinkle over 1 1/2 tablespoons of the eau de vie or cognac. Put 2 more cheese halves on top and repeat these layers until all the ingredients are used up, ending with a layer of cheese and pressing it down well. The cheese should be tightly packed. Sprinkle with the remaining eau de vie or cognac. Pour in enough olive oil to cover the cheese and then leave in a cool place, but not the refrigerator, for at least a week. Store in the refrigerator once opened.

This cheese dip from Hungary is usually made from a soft sheep's milk cheese, which is not always easy to obtain, so I have substituted cream cheese. Crisp crackers are great with this, although a selection of vegetable crudités is also very good. Liptauer keeps for about a week in the refrigerator.

liptauer

SERVES 4

8 ounces cream cheese, such as Philadelphia or fresh Explorateur
$1/4$ cup sour cream
4 tablespoons unsalted butter, softened
2 teaspoons superfine capers, drained
2 canned anchovy fillets, minced
1 tablespoon chopped fresh chives
1 tablespoon mild paprika, plus extra for dusting
1 teaspoon caraway seeds
$1/2$ teaspoon mild mustard
Salt

Blend all the ingredients together briefly in a food processor or beat them together in a bowl. Cover and leave overnight in the refrigerator to let the flavors to infuse. To serve, adjust the seasoning if necessary, transfer to a serving dish, and dust the top with a little paprika.

I love this Lebanese dish, which has been traditionally prepared in the mountain villages for centuries. It is both simple to make and a wonderful appetizer, served with garlic bread or grilled pitta breads.

shanklish

SERVES 4

12 ounces fresh goat cheese
1 garlic clove, minced
1 red hot chili pepper, seeded and minced
2 tablespoons roughly chopped fresh flat-leaf parsley
1 medium red onion, minced
3 ripe but firm tomatoes, cubed
3 tablespoons extra virgin olive oil
Freshly cracked black pepper

Place the goat cheese in a bowl and lightly crush with a fork along with the garlic and chili pepper. Stir in the parsley, onion, and tomato and carefully mix together, taking care not to break up the tomato pieces. Season well with black pepper and transfer to a serving dish. Drizzle over the olive oil and serve.

PG TIPS
In Lebanon and Syria, Shanklish is often mashed with cooked hardboiled egg or with cucumber and mint. Both are equally delicious.

Serve this chutney with a selection of cheeses and some crusty bread. If you are using the sweeter red gooseberries, you will need the smaller amount of sugar listed in the ingredients. Although you can store it in preserving jars for months, a good chutney will also keep for one month unsealed in the refrigerator and will, in fact, improve in flavor.

gooseberry & green peppercorn **chutney**

MAKES ABOUT 2 POUNDS

1½ pounds fresh green or red
  gooseberries
2 onions, chopped
1 garlic clove, minced
½ teaspoon mustard powder
1 teaspoon lemon juice
1¼ cups cider vinegar or
  white wine vinegar
1 heaped cup raisins
½–1½ cups packed brown sugar
A large pinch of salt
2 tablespoons green peppercorns

Put the gooseberries, onions, garlic, mustard and lemon juice in a preserving kettle and pour two-thirds of the vinegar over. Bring to a boil, then reduce the heat and simmer for about 45 minutes, stirring occasionally, until thick. Add the raisins, salt, sugar and the rest of the vinegar. Stir over a low heat until the sugar has dissolved, then simmer for up to 1 hour, stirring frequently, until thick and syrupy. Stir in the peppercorns, then remove from the heat. Either let cool and then store in the refrigerator for up to a month, or pour immediately into hot sterilized jars, seal, process in a boiling-water bath for 10 minutes, and store in a cool, dark place.

The pears are cooked quite briefly so that they keep their shape, resulting in a nice chunky chutney. This chutney is very good served with a mature farmhouse Cheddar.

saffron pear **chutney**

MAKES ABOUT 2 POUNDS

2 apples, peeled & grated
½ cup onions, minced
1 cup golden raisins
Juice & grated zest of 4 oranges
1½ cups sugar
1 teaspoon ground cinnamon
1 teaspoon freshly grated nutmeg
1 teaspoon cayenne pepper
2 pinches of saffron strands

1½ teaspoons salt
¼ cup grated fresh ginger root
1¼ cups white wine vinegar
1¾ pounds pears, peeled, cored &
  roughly chopped
12 ounces tomatoes, skinned,
  seeded & diced

Put all the ingredients except the pears and tomatoes in a preserving kettle and simmer for about 30 minutes, stirring from time to time, until the mixture is reduced to a syrup. It should be thick enough to coat the back of a spoon. Add the pears and tomatoes and cook for 10–15 minutes, until the pears are just soft. Pour into hot sterilized jars, process in a boiling-water bath for 10 minutes, seal, then store in a cool, dark place.

cheeseboard (clockwise from top): capricorn, sainte-maure, keen's cheddar, golden cross, boulettes d'avesnes, roquefort societé, reblochon

A delicately flavored pickle that makes an interesting accompaniment to cheese. Although this recipe uses white grapes, you could substitute red ones. Remember that good-quality vinegar is essential for making a good pickle.

sweet & sour grape **pickle**

MAKES ABOUT 1 QUART

1³/₄ pounds seedless white grapes
10 sprigs of fresh tarragon
2¹/₄ cups champagne vinegar or
  white wine vinegar
³/₄ cup honey
1 teaspoon salt

Wash the grapes well and then dry them. Put them in a large sterilized preserving jar with the sprigs of tarragon. Boil the vinegar and honey together for 2 minutes, then add the salt and pour the mixture over the grapes. Seal the jar immediately. For best results, store in a cool dark place for up to 1 month before opening.

This delicately flavored loaf is one of my favorites and a real winner at the Lanesborough, where we serve it as an accompaniment to our cheese selection. I like it slightly warm with my cheese.

lanesborough dried fig & fennel seed **bread**

MAKES 1 LOAF

1 cake (0.6 ounce) fresh yeast or
  1 package rapid-rise dry yeast
¹/₂ cup water
2 cups whole-wheat flour
¹/₂ teaspoon salt
1 tablespoon unsalted butter
1 cup dried figs, cut into strips
  about ¹/₄ inch wide
1¹/₂ teaspoons fennel seeds

If using fresh yeast, put it in a small bowl, pour on the water and mix until smooth. Put the flour and salt into another bowl and rub in the butter, then make a well in the center and add the yeast and water mixture. Stir in the flour to form a soft dough. If using dry yeast, stir it into the flour after rubbing in the butter and then pour in the water.

Turn the dough out onto a lightly floured surface and knead for 8–10 minutes, until smooth and elastic. Add the dried figs and fennel seeds and knead for 1 minute longer, until incorporated. Do not overknead the dough at this stage or the figs will disintegrate. Let relax for about 5 minutes, then shape into an oval loaf, place on a greased baking sheet, and cover with a clean damp dishtowel. Let rise in a warm place for about 50 minutes, until the loaf has doubled in size.

Preheat the oven to 425°F. Bake the loaf for 30 minutes, or until it is golden brown on top and sounds hollow when tapped on the bottom. Cool on a wire rack.

breads (clockwise from top): stilton bread, mozzarella & sun-dried tomato bread, lanesborough dried fig & fennel seed bread, cheddar & onion loaf, cheddar & onion loaf, stilton bread (center)

index